Authentic Christianity

Starting Strong
and Staying Strong

*Updated with Application Questions
for Each Chapter*

Kim Dean May

Contents

Dedication vii

Acknowledgments ix

Application Question Suggestions xi

Introduction xiii

Chapter 1   Repentance — The Turning
              Point for Salvation 15

Chapter 2   Water Baptism — The Landmark
              for Obedience 21

Chapter 3   Holy Spirit — The Power for
              Christian Living 27

Chapter 4   Discovering God's Will, Part 1 —
              Prayer — Drawing Close
              to God.......................................36

Chapter 5   Discovering God's Will, Part 2 —
                 Fellowship — Developing Christ-
                 Centered Relationships 44

Chapter 6   Discovering God's Will, Part 3 —
                 Scripture — Determining
                 Biblical Guidelines.........................51

Chapter 7   Temptation — The Road of Least
                 Resistance 59

Chapter 8   Trials — The Road of
                 Greatest Purpose 71

Chapter 9   Ministry — Sharing the Love
                 of Christ 86

Chapter 10   Finances — Giving the
                 Blessings of Christ.......................105

Chapter 11   Witnessing — Extending the
                 Truth of Christ..............................122

Chapter 12   Worship — Honoring the
                 Person of Christ............................133

Conclusion 145

Dedication

I dedicate this book to my spiritual mentor, Harold Egli. He was instrumental in helping me get off to a strong start when I became a Christian, a follower of Jesus Christ. He taught me the truth about God, encouraged me to stand firmly devoted to Jesus, and modeled how to rely on the guidance of the Holy Spirit.

I attended a mid-week Bible study at the Egli home. I'll never forget sitting around their large kitchen table, long after the Bible study was over. There I asked question after question, eager to learn more about my newfound faith. Mr. Egli stayed up late into the night, guiding me with scriptural responses.

Getting started in the Christian life was a tremendous joy. And I didn't waver in my dedication to Jesus, which is all too common. I remain strong in Christ over thirty years later. I'm indebted to Mr. Egli for such a steadfast Christian journey.

I hope you will find a mentor like I did. What strength and confidence can be gained from a mature Christian, who nurtures and navigates you along the road of God's will. I also trust this short book will provide clear guidelines for your wonderful adventure as a disciple of Jesus.

Acknowledgements

I extend special appreciation to Dana King, who graciously and diligently edited each chapter prior to the first printing. Thank you to Leo and Dana DeSpain, as well as Bob and Melinda Trose, for generously providing accommodations in which to reflect and write.

I am humbly grateful to Liberty Christian Fellowship and its leaders, who offered sabbatical and ongoing encouragement to complete this work, both initially as well as updates.

Heartfelt thanks go out to my family for always supporting me and my dreams. I give additional thanks to my wife, Bev, who typed the manuscript and sacrificially served me by handling every administrative detail.

And above all, praise be to Jesus Christ in whom is my life and my strength!

Application Questions

Suggestions for Group Leaders

- Be patient with silence, allowing time for reflection.
- Don't explain questions unless clarification is obviously needed.
- Refrain from calling on people, which often makes them feel awkward.
- Ask sensitively for further input when you sense it would be helpful to the group. For example, asking, "Can you tell us more about that?" usually leads to more in-depth discussion.

Suggestions for Individuals

- Answer the chapter questions shortly after reading each chapter.
- Write out your responses.
- Pray about each of your answers, letting God speak to you personally.

- We all have areas in which we need to mature. Consider those areas as you reflect on the questions.

Introduction

I distinctly remember the night a certain young woman visited our Bible Study. During the gathering, some of us gently addressed her need to receive Christ's forgiveness for her sins and to dedicate her life to the Lord. She embraced our message with an open heart and we prayed together, as she seemingly devoted herself to Jesus. Tears of joy streamed down her face, and everyone rejoiced with her. What an amazing time! A few weeks later I discovered this young lady had reverted to her past lifestyle of promiscuity. She went back to the crowd that abused alcohol and drugs. I felt both saddened and shocked. Then my greatest fear was realized — she never returned to Christian fellowship.

As a young Christian, I didn't understand. How could someone ask Jesus to become her Savior and then quickly fall back to sinful ways? I forged through this deep struggle in my soul as God showed me: It is one thing to desire having Jesus, but it is another thing to desire Jesus having us. Lasting devotion occurs only when we let God have complete control of our life. In other words, Jesus cannot be just our Savior. He must be Lord as well.

This book comes from my heart, having seen many derailed from the track of following Christ. Therefore, I want to help you avoid the pitfalls that could endanger your spiritual growth. My prayer is that you would not be like the woman above (or others like her) who lose their spiritual direction somewhere along the Christian path. Instead, I want you to start strong and stay strong for the long haul, as the Bible says, "...Just as you received Christ Jesus as Lord, *continue* to live in him, rooted and built up in him, strengthened ... as you were taught ..." (Colossians 2:6-7) (emphasis mine).

Notice a simple but remarkable truth: The way you begin the Christian life is the way to keep living the Christian life. You can start strong and stay strong! In fact, the fruitfulness of your spiritual pilgrimage directly relates to your initial steps in the journey. It is crucial, then, to experience a great beginning as a follower of Jesus. Like a runner, the way you come out of the starting blocks has a huge impact on how strongly you complete the race.

Authentic Christianity outlines biblical steps for beginning and continuing the Christian life. If you take these steps, you will enjoy a spiritual dynamic that will not lose momentum. Thus, you can finish the race God marked out for you, strong and steadfast, just as you began.

Chapter 1

Repentance

The Turning Point for Salvation

"To do so no more is the truest repentance."
Martin Luther

Repentance marks the first step in the Christian life. It means to turn around. You turn away from your past lifestyle of sinful attitudes and actions, and you turn toward your new lifestyle of godly beliefs and behaviors. Repentance embodies profound change made possible by a soul-stirring choice. You decide to give up control of your life and turn over command to Jesus Christ. Why would you want to relinquish the direction of your future? Because Jesus loves you and designed a masterful blueprint for your life.

Let me explain. God looked upon the sins of mankind. He grieved. His righteousness demanded punishment for all sins, yet He deeply cared for His human creation. What would He do? God entered the earthly sphere in the form of a baby boy, named Jesus. As God in flesh, Jesus grew up with the ultimate purpose of dying on a cross to pay the penalty your sins deserved. He displayed amazing grace, the epitome of sacrifice. The perfect died for the sinful. God lowered Himself to the human level that you might receive forgiveness. Realizing how much He loves you, why wouldn't you give command of your future to Jesus?

Relinquishment of control includes: 1) *realization* — that you were walking contrary to the will of God, 2) *confession* — that you were living under the dominance of sin, and 3) *dedication* — that you now follow after the example of Christ. These elements of repentance comprise the turning point for salvation, as depicted in the following story.

A Young Man's Story

[11]*Jesus continued: "There was a man who had two sons. [12]The younger one said to his father, 'Father, give me my share of the estate.' So he divided his property between them.*

[13]*"Not long after that, the younger son got together all he had, set off for a distant country and there squandered his wealth in wild living. [14]After he had spent everything there was a severe famine in that whole country, and he began to be in need. [15]So he went and hired himself out to a citizen of that country, who sent him to his fields to feed pigs. [16]He*

longed to fill his stomach with the pods that the pigs were eating, but no one gave him anything.

[17] *"When **he came to his senses,** he said, 'How many of my father's hired men have food to spare, and here I am starving to death!* [18]*I will set out and go back to my father and say to him: Father, **I have sinned** against heaven and against you.* [19]*I am no longer worthy to be called your son; make me like one of your hired men.'* [20]*So he got up and went to his father.*

"But while he was still a long way off, his father saw him and was filled with compassion for him; he ran to his son, threw his arms around him and kissed him.

[21] *"The son said to him, 'Father, I have sinned against heaven and against you. I am no longer worthy to be called your son.'*

[22] *"But the father said to his servants, 'Quick! Bring the best robe and put it on him. Put a ring on his finger and sandals on his feet.* [23]*Bring the fattened calf and kill it. Let's have a feast and celebrate.* [24]*For this son of mine was dead and is alive again; he was lost and is found.' So they began to celebrate." (Luke 15:11-24)* (emphasis mine)

The younger son left home to lead a selfish lifestyle, but eventually discovered the foolishness of opposing his father's will. Verse 17 states, "**he came to his senses.**" This was his point of *realization.* Next the son grasped the severity of his attitude and actions. Verse 18 depicts this: "**I have sinned.**" This was his time of *confession.* Finally, the young man returned to his homeland and father, as verse 20 describes, "**so he got up and went to his father**." This was his moment of *dedication.*

Jesus told this story as a clear and concise picture of repentance, the turning point for salvation. It is a change of mind ("he came to his senses") that leads to a change of heart ("I have sinned"), which results in a change of direction ("so he got up and went to his father"). When you give control of your life to God, it involves the same three changes — mind, heart, and direction.

Have you experienced this life-transforming turnaround? If so, you have come back to the place you were meant to be, with your heavenly Father! If not, now is the time to come to your senses. Now is the time to say, "I have sinned against God." Now is the time to return home like the lost son. What hope! God's amazing grace welcomes you into His loving arms, no matter where you've been or what you've done.

Upon repentance, God forgives your sins and accepts you as His child. He promises you an eternal home in heaven. A whole new life, the Christian life, awaits you as well. It's one filled with meaning and adventure.

My Personal Story

I vividly remember my spiritual homecoming on January 24, 1972, the day I surrendered control of my life to God. I lived in stark contrast to God's will. For instance, I knew it was wrong to steal, but did it anyway. I also manipulated people for my own objectives. Furthermore, I developed a habit of drinking and hanging out with friends that used illegal drugs. Like the son Jesus described, I was lost, empty, purposeless.

Then one day an old college friend stopped to visit me as he passed through our town. I hadn't seen or heard from him in many months. I noticed a drastic difference. My friend seemed like a brand new person. His way of talking, his attitude, his behavior, even his countenance had changed. This transformation occurred as a result of repentance. My friend had encountered the love of Christ and experienced a spiritual turnaround.

Yearning for peace and longing for purpose, I called out to God. Admittedly, I wanted what my friend had. As I prayed, I asked the Lord to take command of my life. I wasn't disappointed, for it was my time of realization, confession, and dedication. God welcomed me into His arms of loving acceptance and forgave my sins, transforming me into a new person. The very motivations of my heart shifted heavenward. And I found the supreme purpose for my future, to follow Jesus Christ into the center of God's will. I met head-on the total, perfect, and unconditional love I needed. It was my turning point for salvation.

Application Questions
for Chapter 1 — Repentance

1. Have you experienced the life-transforming turn-around of repentance? If so, describe the circumstances which brought you to the *realization* of your need for Jesus.

2. Where and when did *confession* of your sins occur?

3. Share some personal examples of *dedication* to Christ as your Lord.

4. If you became a Christ-follower at a very early age, how is Jesus evident in your life today? Describe any blessings or struggles you've experienced as a result of making this decision so young.

5. What might be a next step for you as a follower of Jesus?

6. If you have not come to a point of repentance, what could help you move closer?

Chapter 2

Water Baptism

The Landmark for Obedience

*"Baptism is not only an identification
with Christ, but a calling to live the
baptized life." Robert E. Webber*

Obedience to Christ

Your heart opens to God's will as you turn away
from sin and relinquish control to Jesus. You
naturally gravitate to the Lord's plans because you've
experienced Him as a loving Father, knowing He
wants the best for you. The next step God desires is
water baptism. Baptism represents the first command
for a Christian to obey, as observed in the words of
Jesus:

"…All authority in heaven and on earth has been given to me. [19]Therefore, go and make disciples of all nations, baptizing them in the name of the Father and of the Son and of the Holy Spirit, [20]and teaching them to obey everything I have commanded you. And surely I am with you always, to the very end of the age." (Matthew 28:18-20)

Water baptism signaled the initial point of obedience for a Christian in the New Testament. Then, the believer proceeded to learn and obey everything else Jesus taught. Baptism, therefore, is the landmark for obedience. It establishes a precedent for yielding to all other biblical commands.

I have baptized many people as a pastor since 1976. I'll always remember baptizing a family from California, whom my wife and I introduced to Christ in 1978. They realized their need for God, confessed their sinfulness, and dedicated themselves to following Jesus. Their repentance rose from heartfelt conviction. We moved from California not long thereafter. Before we left, though, the father asked me to baptize him and his wife and their three children. It was an unusual day in southern California in that it was raining. Nevertheless, the dad wanted his entire family to be baptized outside in a friend's jacuzzi, rain or no rain.

It was our last night in California. What a blessing to watch these genuine disciples step into the rainy night and be baptized in a hot tub! My soul rejoiced as I took in the significance of the moment. Here, in front of me, stood Christians eager to do what Jesus said. What a picture of authentic Christianity. It is not surprising that decades later they diligently follow all the commands of Jesus. They started strong and remain strong.

Baptism truly sets a pattern for obedience. In addition, other significant reasons for water baptism must be noted. For example, baptism publicly confesses your faith in Christ. It displays an outward sign of an inward change. Baptism declares to your family, friends, church, and community that you love God and are following Jesus as Savior and Lord. What a joyous occasion for others to share in your amazing turnaround!

Identification with Christ

Also, baptism identifies you with the death, burial, and resurrection of Christ. Your immersion in the waters of baptism symbolizes dying to your old life of sin, as Jesus died and was buried in a tomb so you could be free from past transgressions. Your rising out of the waters of baptism represents entry into a new life of righteousness, as Jesus rose from the dead to give you power over future temptations. Romans chapter 6 describes this identification of baptism with the death, burial, and resurrection of Christ:

⁴We were therefore buried with him through baptism into death in order that, just as Christ was raised from the dead through the glory of the Father, we too may live a new life. ⁵If we have been united with him like this in his death, we will certainly also be united with him in his resurrection. ⁶For we know that our old self was crucified with him so that the body of sin might be done away with, that we should no longer be slaves to sin – ⁷because anyone who has died has been freed from sin. (Romans 6:4-7)

New Life in Christ

This passage indicates you have a new life of victory over sin. It does not suggest you will live a perfect life, however. Scripture clarifies that Jesus is the only perfect one. In addition, many verses point out our imperfection as Christians. For example, "If we claim to be without sin, we deceive ourselves and the truth is not in us" (1 John 1:8). At the same time, the encouragement of Romans chapter 6 cannot be underemphasized. Jesus released you from the power of sin. You need not yield any longer to temptation. Whereas sin characterized your old life, obedience is the hallmark of your new life. Water baptism helps start you off strong as the landmark for obedience.

You might wonder, "What happens if I sin?" Here is the answer: "If we confess our sins, He (Christ) is faithful and just and will forgive us our sins and purify us from all unrighteousness" (1 John 1:9). You simply request and accept Christ's forgiveness. Then get back on course with your new life of freedom.

The good news, that sin no longer dominates you, remains rock solid. Sins from the past (or the present) gradually become the exception, not the norm. Because of repentance and water baptism, you now walk on a path of obedience governed by the reign of your God and King, Jesus Christ.

My Baptism

A Lutheran minister baptized me when I was an infant through what is called "sprinkling of water." My parents wanted me to grow up believing and following Christ, and ultimately have a place in heaven. I repented of my sins at age 19. Then I decided to be baptized by immersion in the Atlantic Ocean. This baptism affirmed my parents' godly intentions. Of course, I did not become a Christian through either infant or adult baptism, for salvation only comes by repentance. But my family's hope came to fruition, attested by my immersion in water as a young man. I was a believer in and follower of Jesus, on the road to heaven.

I experienced the meaning of Christian baptism as seen in Romans chapter 6. When immersed, I chose by faith to leave my former sins in the past. They were buried in the ocean even as Jesus buried the power of sin in the tomb. And when I rose out of the water I chose by faith to embrace the new life God planned for me, even as Jesus rose from the dead into a new reality as Risen Lord. How incredible! A life of growing in obedience awaited me.

The same stands true for you as a Christian. You are acquitted of all past sins through repentance and catapulted on the road of obedience through water baptism. But the question remains: How do you advance on this path of godliness?

Application Questions
for Chapter 2 — Water Baptism

1. In what way does water baptism serve as a spiritual landmark?

2. Does the word "obedience" contain a positive or negative connotation for you? Please explain.

3. If you have been baptized, where, when, and how did that take place?

4. How would you describe the significance of baptism in your spiritual journey?

5. If baptized as an infant (or anytime before repentance), what are your thoughts about water baptism by immersion after repentance?

6. If not baptized by immersion after repentance, what might encourage you to do so?

Chapter 3

Holy Spirit

The Power for Christian Living

*"The greatest heresy of the Church of
the present day is unbelief in this Spirit."*
George MacDonald

God does not leave you alone, after repentance and baptism, to figure out the Christian life. As a gracious Father, He gives His Spirit, the Holy Spirit, to empower you into the fullness of His plans. How do you receive the Holy Spirit, the power for Christian living? Let's take a look.

Pattern

Suppose you enter my office right now, as I am writing this book, and inquire how to become a Christian. I would tell you about the need to repent as outlined in the first chapter. After you realized your need, confessed your sin, and dedicated your life to the Lord, I would teach you the significance of water baptism as explained in Chapter 2. Then I'd schedule a time for you to be baptized. This would happen as soon as possible, ideally the next Sunday your family and friends could come to witness your change of mind, heart, and direction. Afterwards (although this can occur before water baptism), I would pray for you to receive the gift of the Holy Spirit. I'd ask God to fill you with His Spirit as the authority and power for Christian living.

What a transformational launch onto the biblical course of following Christ! You have been cleansed from past sins, abandoned your old life in the waters of baptism, and empowered by the Holy Spirit to lay hold of your new life as a disciple of Jesus. Indeed, you cannot follow the example of Christ in your own strength. God exhibits lovingkindness, then, in gifting you with His Holy Spirit so you can accomplish His holy will.

Repentance, water baptism, and the Holy Spirit comprise a three-fold scriptural pattern. The apostle Peter linked these three components together when he preached to the crowds at Pentecost: "…Repent and be baptized, every one of you, in the name of Jesus Christ for the forgiveness of your sins. And you will receive the gift of the Holy Spirit" (Acts 2:38). This three-fold combination furnishes not only an historic sermon, but the biblical pattern for your initial strides on the pathway of Christianity. God constructed this road to provide a strong and stable beginning to your spiritual journey.

Dilemma

Unfortunately, not every Christian's experience lines up with the Acts 2:38 pattern. For example, no one instructed me about the value and need for baptism by immersion until some time after my repentance. Therefore, it was delayed for six months. It could have occurred (and should have occurred) within hours or days of relinquishing control of my life to God. Yes, my baptism proved meaningful, but the unnecessary wait set back its spiritual impact.

In addition, I experienced confusion about Peter's words, "… You will receive the gift of the Holy Spirit." The Spirit obviously directed the process of repentance, convicting me of sinfulness and the need for righteousness. Why did I need to receive this gift of God, if the Spirit was already working in me?

Eventually, God clarified this issue and answered my question. First, He showed me in the book of Acts that some new Christians received the Holy Spirit separate from the moment of repentance and/ or water baptism. The Samaritans serve as unmistakable examples:

[12]But when they believed Philip as he preached the good news of the kingdom of God and the name of Jesus Christ, they were baptized, both men and women. [13]Simon himself believed and was baptized.

And he followed Philip everywhere, astonished by the great signs and miracles he saw.

[14]*When the apostles in Jerusalem heard that Samaria had accepted the word of God, they sent Peter and John to them.* [15]*When they arrived, they prayed for them that they might receive the Holy Spirit,* [16]*because the Holy Spirit had not yet come upon any of them; they had simply been baptized into the name of the Lord Jesus.* [17]*Then Peter and John placed their hands on them, and they received the Holy Spirit. (Acts 8:12-17)*

The Samaritans repented and were baptized (vs. 12). Surely the Holy Spirit worked in their hearts and influenced their decisions for salvation and subsequent immersion. However, "because the Holy Spirit had not yet come upon any of them" (vs. 16), Peter and John were commissioned to pray for these new believers. They placed their hands on them as they prayed, "and they received the Holy Spirit" (vs. 17). This scenario plainly demonstrates a repentant and baptized follower of Christ may have yet to receive the Holy Spirit as God fully intends.

Conversely, I found some receive the Holy Spirit immediately upon repentance, to the full measure of God's will. Cornelius and his family represent this reality:

[23]*… The next day Peter started out with them, and some of the brothers from Joppa went along.* [24]*The following day he arrived in Caesarea. Cornelius was*

expecting them and had called together his relatives and close friends.

⁴⁴While Peter was still speaking these words, the Holy Spirit came on all who heard the message. ⁴⁵The circumcised believers who had come with Peter were astonished that the gift of the Holy Spirit had been poured out even on the Gentiles. ⁴⁶For they heard them speaking in tongues and praising God.

Then Peter said, ⁴⁷"Can anyone keep these people from being baptized with water? They have received the Holy Spirit just as we have." ⁴⁸So he ordered that they be baptized in the name of Jesus Christ. Then they asked Peter to stay with them for a few days. (Acts 10:23-24, 44-48)

God instructed the apostle Peter to visit Cornelius. Cornelius, in turn, was directed by God to gather his family and friends to hear Peter proclaim the gospel. Something powerful happened as Peter preached the good news of Christ, even before he could finish his message! Cornelius and those gathered in his home received the Holy Spirit: "… the Holy Spirit came on all who heard the message" (vs. 44). Peter acknowledged this: "… they have received the Holy Spirit just as we have" (vs. 47).

Here the light turned on in my understanding. Some receive the Holy Spirit when they repent. Others receive the Holy Spirit sometime (usually soon) after they repent. I understood Acts 2:38 as the God-given pattern for new Christians, i.e., God wants everyone to repent, be baptized, and receive the Holy Spirit. Now I also realized God brings His pattern to fruition in different ways with different people. The God of creation works creatively with each individual. Thus, the paramount question is not, "How, or when, did you receive the Holy Spirit?" Rather, it is "Have you received the Holy Spirit to the degree God desires?"

Therefore, when I pray for people to receive the Spirit of God, I aim to be sensitive, not manipulative. First, I recognize the Holy Spirit is already present and operative in all believers. Scripture asserts this, "… if anyone does not have the spirit of Christ, he does not belong to Christ" (Romans 8:9). Second, I inquire about their experience. For instance, do they identify with the Samaritans in Acts chapter 8 or Cornelius in Acts chapter 10?

If their experience parallels the Samaritans, I respectfully seek permission to pray for them like Peter and John did for those in Samaria. I simply and gently ask God to fill them to the measure He desires. At minimum, they've tasted the Holy Spirit. Now they enjoy the feast of God's life-giving presence and power. On the other hand, some people identify with Cornelius. They were filled to overflowing with God's Spirit in an undeniable manner at the moment they heard and accepted the message of Christ. As a result, they don't need another Christian to pray for them concerning the Holy Spirit.

Looking back, I relate to Cornelius. My life dramatically changed the very day I surrendered control to Jesus. I was inspired to pray, read the Bible, fellowship with Christians, sing songs of worship to God, and tell others about my Savior and Lord. Most of all, I loved Jesus and longed to do His will regardless of the cost. Clearly, I received the Spirit in the biblical pattern of Acts 2:38, which unleashed in me the power for Christian living.

Whether you experience the Spirit like the Samaritans or Cornelius, "Holy Spirit reception" results from pure trust in God. No prerequisites exist, only repentance. You candidly request and God kindly imparts. "How much more will your Father in heaven give the Holy Spirit to those who ask Him" (Luke 11:13).

God doesn't consult anyone about how and when He pours out His Spirit from heaven. You just ask. Then be assured He will fulfill His promise. The same is true throughout your Christian life. The Holy Spirit initiates all the blessings of God, apart from human insight, planning, and timeliness. The Holy Spirit is God's Spirit and He releases His Spirit as He sees fit. He does whatever He wants, whenever He desires, however He chooses.

Change

Expect wonderful changes as the Holy Spirit takes charge of your life, especially the maturation of your character. This transpires through the development of what scripture calls "the fruit of the Spirit." Spiritual fruit consists of "... love, joy, peace, patience, kindness, goodness, faithfulness, gentleness, and self-control ..." (Galatians 5:22-23). Generally speaking, these character qualities profile the attributes of God. The Spirit cultivates godly fruit in your character as a natural by-product of a heart rooted in the good ground of the gospel message. Be patient, then, and follow the guidelines of this book, and most importantly the Bible. You won't be disappointed for, little by little, season by season, you will mature in the likeness of your holy God through the Holy Spirit.

The Holy Spirit is the power for Christian living, yet some questions need to be answered. For example, how do I determine each step of my Christian pilgrimage? How do I know when I'm not on track with God's purpose? In essence, how do I know God's will? Chapter 4 will unveil answers to these compelling questions.

Application Questions
for Chapter 3 — Holy Spirit

1. What were you taught about the Holy Spirit in your youth? What about recently?

2. Share any lingering confusion you have about the Spirit of God.

3. Do you identify moreso with the experience of the Samaritans in Acts 8 or with Cornelius in Acts 10? Please explain.

4. Would you like someone, or a group of Christians, to pray for you to receive the Holy Spirit like Peter and John did for the Samaritan believers? If so, who will you ask?

5. What do you consider the major change in your character since the Holy Spirit took control of your life?

Chapter 4

Discovering God's Will
Part 1 – Prayer

Drawing Close to God

"Prayer is not monologue, but dialogue."
Andrew Murray

Y ou are now equipped with the presence of the
Holy Spirit, so you can powerfully run the
Christian race. But how do you know which way to
run? Direction to the heart of God's will is revealed
by following three guidelines — prayer, fellowship,
and scripture. You progressively comprehend God's
design for your future as you communicate with
Him, interact with other Christians, and reflect on
the truths of the Bible. Let's begin with the guideline
of prayer.

Communicating with God

Prayer entails consistent and open communication with God. This communication includes personal requests, as Jesus encouraged when He said, "Ask and it will be given to you; seek and you will find; knock and the door will be opened to you. For everyone who asks receives; he who seeks finds; and to him who knocks, the door will be opened" (Matthew 7:7-8). God loves to provide everything you need.   However, you may ask God for something and no answer seems apparent. Why? Sometimes this is the reason: "When you ask, you do not receive, because you ask with wrong motives ..." (James 4:3). God almost always withholds a request motivated by selfishness. Whether the reason consists of wrong motives or something else, unanswered prayer affords an opportunity to learn about yourself and mature in your understanding of God's will.

Consider the day I lost my job, when my employer suddenly decided to go out of business. I was stunned! I managed a Christian bookstore while attending graduate school full-time. My wife was preparing to leave her job because our first child was due in a few weeks. My income enabled us to pay for our house, cars, my education, and all other living expenses. We would be in deep financial trouble unless I found employment immediately. Therefore, I searched every possibility. I applied for work as a painter, a waiter, a security guard, any job that would allow me to take care of my family. But no one would hire me.

I drove home one afternoon following another unproductive day of standing in long lines seeking employment. Surprisingly, this thought popped into my mind: "Maybe I'm not supposed to have one of these jobs; maybe God has something different for me." The idea caught me off guard. As I reflected, however, I sensed this could actually be God's will. Possibly He had been shielding me from obtaining one of these jobs because He had some other type of work in store for me.

I spent significant time praying the next few days. Drawing close to God, I poured out my soul to Him. Then I listened, and He communicated His will to my heart. God wanted me to return to full-time pastoral ministry. I worked as a pastor for a few years, but left church ministry to gain the necessary education to become a psychologist. However, this career change was my choosing, not the Lord's. Now I discerned His gentle voice directing me, even correcting me as the Holy Spirit brought this verse to mind: "For my thoughts are not your thoughts, neither are your ways my ways," declares the Lord (Isaiah 55:8).

Oh, what a valuable learning curve. God invites us to pray and gladly provides everything we need. He also realigns us with His purpose when our ways are not His ways. Even when it seems like our prayers are unheard, our gracious heavenly Father guides us in the discovery of His will. In my case, God's will not only renewed my pastoral ministry, He renewed me! And just as important, He led me to the underlying nature of prayer: drawing close to Him in a relationship of two-way communication.

Listening to God

As seen in the story above, listening to God forms the second half of prayer. How does this happen? You simply talk to God, and He talks to you. In addition to presenting requests to God, you permit the Lord time to speak into your heart. Jesus said, "My sheep listen to my voice; I know them, and they follow me" (John 10:27). Listening to God equals, and probably exceeds, the significance of talking to God.

Two results (observed in John 10:27) occur when you listen to God through your Shepherd, Jesus Christ. The first result of listening is intimacy: "I know them." God eagerly desires closeness with you. He does not want an impersonal relationship consisting of routine prayer requests. Rather, He prefers a one-on-one relationship of heartfelt interaction. Therefore, don't let your prayers turn into a shopping list you carry to God. Instead, take ample time to listen to the Lord's voice as well as articulating your needs to Him. The interaction of your concerns and His responses draws you close together. Thus, prayer creates a two-way relationship of loving communication, a full circle of spiritual intimacy.

The second result of listening is obedience: "They follow me." You can't fully obey God's will until you hear Him speak to your heart. Obedience, then, springs out of listening to the Lord and ensuing intimacy with Him. Jesus spent regular time alone with the Father, an example watched closely by the disciples. One time they asked, "Lord, teach us to pray" (Luke 11:1). They hungered for what Jesus enjoyed — intimacy with God and obedience to God.

The model prayers of Christ definitely included both speaking and listening. And the listening aspect of prayer was key to His obedience to the Father: "… the Son can do nothing by himself; he can do only what he sees his Father doing …" (John 5:19). "I do nothing on my own but speak just what the Father has taught me" (John 8:28). Jesus did not assume initiative apart from God's directives. He saw what His Father was wanting and heard what His Father was saying. This was normative in His prayer times of two-way communication. Subsequently, Christ only did what God was doing and only said what God was saying. Jesus obviously sustained a life of obedience as a result of drawing close to the Father through listening.

You can listen to the Lord when you finish talking to Him, or intermingled with your prayers. Then, test whatever you sense God speaks to your heart. You might ask, "is this wisdom?" What you hear in prayer is wisdom from your Father in heaven if it contains godly attributes. The apostle James paints a picture of receiving true wisdom from God: "But the wisdom that comes from heaven is first of all pure; then peace-loving, considerate, submissive, full of mercy and good fruit, impartial and sincere" (James 3:17). If the impressions on your heart come from God, they will be filled with godly wisdom.

Therefore, they will be pure, peace-loving, considerate, etc.

"Is this biblical?" formulates a second question to ask yourself. The Bible supplies the objectivity by which you measure the legitimacy of anything heard in prayer. "All scripture is God-breathed and is useful for teaching, rebuking, correcting and training in righteousness" (2 Timothy 3:16). What you believe God might be saying must align itself with the Bible. If not, get rid of it because God's will does not violate God's Word. I will elaborate on the practical nature of scripture in discovering God's will when we reach Chapter 6.

Application

Here are a few suggestions to make prayer a significant part of your daily life. Consider the following acrostic:

P - **P**rime time: Pray when your energy level is up.
R - **R**egular time: Pray at a set time each day.
A - **A**lone time: Pray somewhere without distractions.
Y - **Y**ielded time: Pray with a pliable heart.

As a follower of Jesus, be encouraged! Take healthy advantage of the opportunity to converse with the Creator of the world. Tell Him your concerns and needs. Listen to Him as well, for you cannot know a person to whom you have not listened. Let your communication be a communion, a union of your heart with His heart. This will create intimacy with God and obedience to God, two characteristics that develop in the context of prayer and release you into further discovery of His will. Let's look now at another critical area in the pursuit of God's marvelous plans.

Application Questions for Chapter 4 — Discovering God's Will, Part 1

1. What does prayer look like in your relationship with God?

2. How have you learned to listen to God in prayer? What else could assist you in "tuning in" to His voice?

3. Tell about a scenario when someone supposedly heard God's voice, but the message did not agree with scripture. How was this counter-productive or even hurtful?

4. Tell about a time when someone really did hear God's voice. What benefit occurred?

5. Using "PRAY" as an acrostic, write down an action plan to make prayer a significant part of your daily life.

Chapter 5

Discovering God's Will
Part 2 – Fellowship

Developing Christ-Centered Relationships

"The Bible knows nothing of solitary religion."
John Wesley

Interdependence

The second guideline for discovering God's will is fellowship, which involves close inter-personal relationship rooted in mutual devotion to Christ. It is not merely attending the same church or participating in a shared activity. Fellowship encompasses much more. It includes opening your heart to trustworthy Christians, sharing with one another the vital issues of life, like current decisions and future aspirations. You also disclose areas of utmost concern such as needs, problems, temptations, and weaknesses. You encourage and pray for one another in these Christ-centered relationships, and assist each other in practical ways. The goal? Staying on course with God's will in every situation.

Fellowship evolves through understanding how much you need others and others need you. This principle of caring relationship appears throughout scripture, mirroring Christ's command to love one another. The following biblical metaphor describes the loving, interdependent nature of the church:

[12]*The body is a unit, though it is made up of many parts; and though all its parts are many, they form one body. So it is with Christ.*

[14]*Now the body is not made up of one part but of many.* [15]*If the foot should say, "Because I am not a hand, I do not belong to the body," it would not for that reason cease to be part of the body.* [16]*And if the ear should say, "Because I am not an eye, I do not belong to the body," it would not for that reason cease to be part of the body.* [17]*If the whole body were an eye, where would the sense of hearing be? If the whole body were an ear, where would the sense of smell be?* [18]*But in fact God has arranged the parts in the body, every one of them, just as he wanted them to be.* [19]*If they were all one part, where would the body be?* [20]*As it is, there are many parts, but one body.* (1 Corinthians 12:12, 14-20)*

As the physical body contains many intercon-nected parts, so the spiritual body (the church) includes many interwoven members. Each part of the

physical body joins and works together in cohesive-
ness and coordination, resulting in maximum effectiveness. The same is true of the church. The body
of Christ maximizes its effectiveness by its interdependent nature. Put simply, you were made to know
and do God's will alongside your brothers and sisters
in Christ. In order to fulfill its purpose, an arm con-
nects to and functions with the shoulder, wrist, hand,
and fingers. So you also come together in unity with
other parts of Christ's body to fulfill what you were
meant for — God's will!

Support

A host of benefits emerge from the interdependent makeup of Christ-centered relationships. One is
support. I remember the news reporting an unusu-
ally heavy and wet snowfall that hit North Carolina
a few years ago. Large groves of tall pine trees lined
one particular interstate. Their branches, bowed from
the weight of the snow, leaned against each other for
mutual support. Trees that stood alone, however,
looked quite different. In fact, their branches snapped
from the pressure of the snowfall, some strewn on
the frozen ground. These pines had no other trees in
proximity to lend support.

Like the beautiful pines of North Carolina,
you need others closeby. Why? Because no one is
immune to the storms of life. When heavy circumstances try to weigh you down, fellowship will keep
you standing strong, preventing discouragement and
defeat. Solomon, considered the wisest man in the

world, said it like this: "Though one may be over-powered, two can defend themselves. A cord of three strands is not quickly broken" (Ecclesiastes 4:12). Such strength generates from mutually supportive, Christ-centered relationships. Remain a healthy branch, then, by staying closely connected to caring Christians who weather storms hand-in-hand, and together persevere in the will of God.

Fellowship Groups

Interdependent relationships develop best through regular gatherings in a home setting with like-minded Christians. The New Testament church provides a model of these fellowship groups, or what is commonly called "small groups" or "cell groups" today: "Every day they continued to meet together in the temple courts. They broke bread in their homes and ate together with glad and sincere hearts" (Acts 2:46).

The early church embraced genuine fellowship. They met not only in the temple area for larger con-gregational services, but also in believers' homes for smaller fellowship gatherings. The focus of these small groups included prayer, communion, worship, and even sharing material resources (Acts 2:42-47). Just imagine the support and strength that permeated these Christ-centered relationships. No wonder "they devoted themselves ... to the fellowship ..." (Acts 2:42).

Participation in worship services and other major gatherings of your church is crucial. Here you receive instruction from your spiritual leaders and understand the direction in which they are shepherding the church. But you gain spiritual courage and confidence in a unique way through a fellowship group that draws close to God by drawing close to one another. Nothing can substitute for mutual encouragement in a small group that seeks and heeds God's will. Therefore, find a church that places high value on fellowship and maintains a strong ministry of small groups. Here are a few suggestions:

- Ask leaders to recommend a possible group(s) for you.
- Take time to know and trust group members.
- Share your needs discreetly and succinctly.
- Prioritize listening to and praying for others.
- Offer your spiritual gifts gently and respectfully.
- Encourage your small group leaders consistently.
- Serve group members as opportunities arise.
- Thank God for the blessings of fellowship.

God's Will

I can attest repeatedly how fellowship enables the discovery of God's will. One group night remains forever etched in my memory. We gathered for worship, prayer, sharing, and study of scripture. At an appropriate time, a man spoke a message of encouragement to me. He said God planned to give me the gift of teaching and work through me in a mighty way. He also asserted that God's blessing would become increasingly apparent in the years ahead as I instructed people in the truths of scripture.

Never in my life was I so inspired and motivated. I left that gathering with a conviction in my heart that nothing would be impossible if I remained faithful to the Lord. The proverb came alive: "As iron sharpens iron, so one man sharpens another" (Proverbs 27:17). That evening God sharpened me with a profound understanding of His will for my future. It was one man sharpening another, to be an instrument in God's hand. This life-changing encouragement took place in the intimate circle of a small group fellowship.

Stay prayerful to know divine guidance. At the same time, realize that "plans fail for lack of counsel, but with many advisers they succeed" (Proverbs 15:22). The dynamic of fellowship hones your ability to perceive God's direction. You may receive insight in your times alone praying for spiritual guidance. Nevertheless, you also need caring relationships in the church in order to navigate the course of God's will. You just can't do it by yourself, but with many advisers you will succeed. Be encouraged, then, to build Christ-centered relationships, for interdependence is biblical and fellowship essential to walk out God's purposes. Now, let's explore the final guideline for discovering God's will.

Application Questions for Chapter 5 — Discovering God's Will, Part 2

1. Why is fellowship so important?

2. Have you participated in a church-based small group or other type of fellowship group? If so, what did group times look like? What type of group most appeals to you now?

3. Share some joys you experienced in a small group setting.

4. How did fellowship assist you in knowing God's will (in a particular situation or life in general)?

5. What are some things to consider before sharing with another person what you believe is an impression from the Lord?

6. If not currently in a group, what would encourage you to start attending one?

Chapter 6

Discovering God's Will
Part 3 — Scripture

Determining Biblical Guidelines

"Apply yourself wholly to the Scriptures, and apply the Scriptures wholly to yourself." Bengel

The Final Test

The third avenue for discovering God's will is scripture. Guidance received from prayer and fellowship must agree with the truth of the Bible. Why? Because everyone is human and capable of mistakes. First, you can misread God as you listen to Him in prayer. For example, you may want something so much that it appears to be God's will. However, your conclusion may reflect your own desire.

Also, you can receive counsel from fellowship that doesn't represent true wisdom. Someone may eagerly hope to bless you with words of encouragement. They truly care, but their input could spring from good intentions rather than God's initiative. The direction they want you to take might bypass God's road. Good advice sometimes differs from God's wisdom.

The ideas you glean from prayer and the input you acquire in fellowship may prove faulty, then, because they are subjective in nature. However, the truth of scripture is objective, not subject to error. As mentioned at the end of Chapter 4, "All Scripture is God-breathed ..." (2 Timothy 3:16). The Bible is inspired by God, perfect and infallible because it emanates from His righteousness. The Word of God abides as the objective will of God, pure and blameless.

Be careful, then, of making decisions based only on prayer and fellowship. Enjoy the safety of submitting your choices to the flawless nature of scripture. Let the Bible, as the ultimate test for understanding God's will, finalize the decision-making process. If what you hear in prayer and fellowship is not congruent with God's Word, it's time to reevaluate. On the other hand, if it stands in harmony with the Bible, have confidence to move forward. Authentic Christianity demands agreement with scripture, because God's Word is the exact standard for knowing God's will.

Failing the Test

I have frequently seen Christians fall short of God's will as revealed in scripture. Consider sexual purity. A couple may truly love each other. As they pray about their relationship, though, they do not hear God's voice, because it is drowned out by the loud calls of their sexual desires. Soon they dismiss the uncompromising commands of scripture to be holy. Instead, they justify a sexual relationship outside of marriage as a natural expression of genuine love. Searching for assurance, they find a like-minded person to affirm their sexual involvement as okay.

At this point, they devalue the Bible (although they would likely not admit it). The Word of God no longer embodies objective truth for them to obey, but relative truth for them to rationalize. As a result, they cannot profess, "I delight in your decrees; I will not neglect your word" (Psalm 119:16). Sadly, they fail the test of scripture by ignoring biblical guidelines such as: "It is God's will that you should be sanctified: that you should avoid sexual immorality; that each of you should learn to control his own body in a way that is holy and honorable" (1 Thessalonians 4:3-4). Consequently, they give way to sin and miss the mark of God's will.

Word and Will

The Word of God defines the will of God. Admittedly, the Bible does not function as a text book, filled with black and white formulas for every situation you encounter. It doesn't say, "Thou shalt not smoke cigarettes." Nonetheless, scripture provides spiritual commands plus spiritual principles that reveal the character and purpose of God. Relevant to smoking, the Bible does say, "Don't you know that you yourselves are God's temple and that God's Spirit lives in you? If anyone destroys God's temple, God will destroy him …" (1 Corinthians 3:16-17).

These verses, along with many others, tell you to honor your physical body in which God has taken residence by His Spirit. Knowing this principle of caring for your body enables you to decide if smoking cigarettes fits with God's will. Direction oftentimes is not spelled out in a specific command, but in a general principle. Whether a distinct command or a guiding principle, the Word of God prescribes the will of God. "Your word is a lamp to my feet and a light for my path" (Psalm 119:105).

Passing the Test

Many biblical heroes, like Peter, model obedience to God's words. He was a fisherman by trade. One morning he returned from a full night of work, unproductive and unsuccessful. He hadn't caught one fish. Jesus spoke to Peter, "Put out into deep water, and let down the nets for a catch" (Luke 5:4). Peter responded, "Because you say so, I will let down the nets" (Luke 5:5).

Tired from a long night out on the water, Peter likely felt discouraged. He knew he didn't have to go back out on the lake. He could have easily gone home to eat breakfast and get some sleep. Getting back in the boat opposed rational sense, but Peter resumed fishing simply because Jesus said so.

Moreover, Jesus was a carpenter, not a fisherman. When Peter took a fishing lesson from a carpenter, he passed the test. He obeyed the word of the Lord as the will of the Lord. The result? "When they had done so, they caught such a large number of fish that their nets began to break" (Luke 5:6).

A Humble Heart

Peter exemplified a humble heart. Approach the Bible with the same attitude: "humbly accept the word planted in you ..." (James 1:21). Be willing to do whatever God tells you. Don't merely listen to the words of the Lord in scripture. Obey them and you will be blessed like Peter, for you have this promise: "...The man who looks intently into the perfect law that gives freedom, and continues to do this, not forgetting what he has heard, but doing it — he will be blessed in what he does" (James 1:25).

Living humbly within the delightful parameters of scripture firmly places you under the hand of God's blessing. Consider this analogy. The Bible is to the will of God what a steering wheel is to a car. A steering wheel is the primary instrument to direct your route. It keeps you on the street and affords you safe travel. As a steering wheel leads a vehicle along the road, humbly allow scripture to lead you into the will of God. There you will find protection and blessing. Peter learned this lesson well. Later in life he wrote, "Humble yourselves, therefore, under God's mighty hand ..." (1 Peter 5:6). A humble heart, yielding to the guidance of scripture, is a tell-tale sign of authentic Christianity.

Living the Scripture

Since the Word of God defines the will of God, you cannot know God's will apart from an understanding of His Word. Therefore, diligently study the scriptures. Here are some suggestions for grasping scriptural commands and principles, and then determining biblical guidelines for all your important decisions.

1. **Read daily** — Reading the Bible every day gives you continual insight to know and choose God's will. "But his delight is in the law of the Lord, and on his law he meditates day and night" (Psalm 1:2).
2. **Study thoroughly** — Reflecting numerous times on a passage of scripture plants its counsel more deeply in your heart. "I meditate on your precepts and consider your ways. ... Your statutes are my delight; they are my counselors" (Psalm 119:15, 24).
3. **Memorize regularly** — Memorizing the word of God strengthens resistance against temptations that entice you away from God's purposes. "I have hidden your word in my heart that I might not sin against you" (Psalm 119:11).
4. **Inquire frequently** — Asking questions of spiritually mature Christians (especially a

small group leader or pastor) provides safety as you interpret God's will from scripture. "The way of a fool seems right to him, but a wise man listens to advice" (Proverbs 12:15).

5. **Apply constantly** — Putting the Word of God into practice reinforces its practical nature and transforming power to keep you in God's will. "This has been my practice: I obey your precepts" (Psalm 119:56). "Therefore everyone who hears these words of mine and puts them into practice is like a wise man who built his house on the rock" (Matthew 7:24).

You will know the plans of God with relative ease if you follow these suggestions closely. Yes, pray and listen to the Lord. Yes, seek wisdom as you fellowship with other Christians. But whatever you do, esteem scripture as the objective and ultimate test for discovering God's will. With the Bible as your guide, you can prevail on God's path regardless of the challenges. You'll see how in the next two chapters.

Application Questions for Chapter 6 — Discovering God's Will, Part 3

1. Why must our decisions and direction align with scripture?

2. If you have a favorite Bible passage, what is it? Why is it your favorite?

3. Relate a course of action you took because of biblical guidance. What were the results?

4. Share a decision you made that went against the standard of scripture. What were the results?

5. In what area of your life has biblical clarity been difficult to find?

6. What change would enable you to study the Bible more regularly or apply it more consistently? What will it take to implement that change?

Chapter 7

Temptation

The Road of Least Resistance

*"The thing that makes men and rivers
crooked is following the line of least resistance."*
Anonymous

Everyone is Tempted

The directives of prayer, fellowship, and scripture promise an exciting adventure of living in God's will. At the same time, authentic Christianity doesn't create a life without problems. Unfortunately, Christians (especially new believers) sometimes buy into the myth that following Jesus precludes difficulties. But no one secures an exemption from temptations and trials. Keep in mind that Jesus Himself encountered temptation.

¹Then Jesus was led by the Spirit into the desert to be tempted by the devil. ²After fasting forty days and forty nights, he was hungry. ³The tempter came to him and said, "If you are the Son of God, tell these stones to become bread."

⁴Jesus answered, "It is written: 'Man does not live on bread alone, but on every word that comes from the mouth of God.'"

⁵ Then the devil took him to the holy city and had him stand on the highest point of the temple. ⁶"If you are the Son of God," he said, "throw yourself down. For it is written: 'He will command his angels concerning you, and they will lift you up in their hands, so that you will not strike your foot against a stone.'"

⁷Jesus answered him, "It is also written: 'Do not put the Lord your God to the test.'" ⁸Again, the devil took him to a very high mountain and showed him all the kingdoms of the world and their splendor. ⁹"All this I will give you," he said, "if you will bow down and worship me."

¹⁰Jesus said to him, "Away from me, Satan! For it is written: 'Worship the Lord your God, and serve him only.'" ¹¹Then the devil left him, and angels came and attended him. (Matthew 4:1-11)

These temptations occurred right after Christ's water baptism (Matthew 3:13-17) and right before His public ministry (Matthew 4:12-22). Just getting started, Jesus was confronted by spiritual opposition.

The Nature of Temptation

All three temptations Jesus faced involved self-ishness. The devil offered food to meet the hunger Jesus experienced while fasting (vs. 3). Satan suggested a dramatic event that would unnecessarily draw attention to Christ (vs. 6). And the tempter guaranteed riches to lure Jesus away from worshipping God (vs. 9). Each temptation pointed down the road of least resistance, the way of selfishness. But Jesus knew His ultimate purpose on earth meant death on a cross. Sure it would have been much easier to accept Satan's "shortcuts" around the cross. However, Christ addressed these spiritual traps and walked right past them. Nothing (not food, popularity, or wealth) would prevent Him from fulfilling His destiny.

Satan tempts you like he tempted Jesus. He solicits you to buy into the road of least resistance, the way that expresses selfish desire to the expense of selfless obedience. The devil schemes to distract and discourage you with "shortcuts", which are actually detours from God's plan for your future. Be aware, then, that any thought promoting your selfish will is a temptation, and any thought opposing God's holy will is a temptation.

Many years ago the temptation of resentment confronted me. A close friend and co-worker treated me unfairly. I felt deeply hurt. Eventually, I left that place of employment. However, my emotions didn't leave me. My hurt turned to anger, and I was left with two choices. First, I could take the selfish way out and avoid all contact with my friend. On the other hand, I could forgive him for hurting me and attempt to reestablish communication.

The first choice presented the road of least resistance. I could hold fast to my justifiable anger and put no effort into the work of forgiveness and reconciliation. The other option required the difficult course of obedience. I decided to face my anger and forgive. I sidestepped the trap of bitterness by initiating a meeting with my friend, expressing that I cared about him and held nothing against him. It wasn't easy, but it was God's holy will. The result? Selfishness, the nature of temptation, suffered defeat just as it did on the day Jesus was tempted three times in the desert.

Temptation versus Sin

Temptations are common and normal. Selfish and unholy thoughts entice everyone. These thoughts, though, do not equate to sin. Jesus experienced temptation and yet remained perfect. Temptation only becomes sin if you embrace and entertain the enticing idea. Temptation does not give birth to sin if you choose to reject and renounce the selfish thought. Therefore, sin is not a matter of what comes into your mind, but it is a matter of what you do with what comes into your mind.

If you permit the temptation to seep into your heart, then it evolves into sin. For example, Jesus proclaimed, "You have heard that it was said, 'Do not commit adultery.' But I tell you that anyone who looks at a woman lustfully has already committed adultery with her in his heart" (Matthew 5:27-28). The word "looks" means to look and keep on looking. The enticing idea to commit adultery creates a temptation, not a sin. But if that tempting thought grows into a longing of your heart, then sin develops.

The Sinful Nature

The devil tempts you through your sinful nature. Sometimes the Bible refers to the sinful nature as the fleshly nature or the old nature. This part of you remains vulnerable to sin. The sinful nature does not disappear or become inoperative after your turn-around experience of repentance. It exists as the selfish side of your humanity, capable of many behaviors that are offensive to God. "The acts of the sinful nature are obvious: sexual immorality, impurity and debauchery; idolatry and witchcraft; hatred, discord, jealousy, fits of rage, selfish ambition, dissensions, factions and envy; drunkenness, orgies, and the like …" (Galatians 5:19-21).

The sinful nature co-exists with your spiritual nature in Christ, referred to in the Bible as the divine nature or the new nature. The sinful nature and spiritual nature battle against each other. This explains why you feel internal tension at times. While enticed by your old nature to choose what is sinful, you are prompted by your new nature to choose what is righteous. This internal tension feels like a tug-of-war.

Words often form the battleground for this spiritual war. Suppose you and a friend are talking about a mutual acquaintance who is absent during the conversation. Suddenly, you think critically about the acquaintance. Then you hesitate. You recognize the inappropriateness of speaking this criticism which is on the tip of your tongue. You might even wonder, "Would I want someone to make these remarks about me, behind my back?"

Another part of you thinks, "Don't worry about it. You're only stating the obvious. No big deal! Besides, you have the right to your opinion." This tension depicts the ongoing war between your new nature and your old nature. Your new nature is kind and caring like Christ. The old nature can readily be critical, even cruel.

Fortunately, victory awaits you. You never lose the freedom and power of choosing to follow the divine nature of Christ. As a Christian, you can avoid the acts of the sinful nature and participate in the righteous nature of Jesus. Your godly choices will ultimately produce the fruit of the Spirit mentioned in Chapter 3: "… love, joy, peace, patience, kindness, goodness, faithfulness, gentleness and self-control" (Galatians 5:22-23).

Resisting Temptation

Returning to Matthew 4:1-11, you see how Jesus resisted temptation, countering each one with scripture: "It is written: 'Man does not live on bread alone, but on every word that comes from the mouth of God'" (vs. 4). "It is also written: 'Do not put the Lord your God to the test'" (vs. 7). "Away from me,

Satan! For it is written: 'Worship the Lord your God, and serve him only'" (vs. 10).

Like Christ, your weapon to resist the power of the enemy is the truth of the Bible. Jesus studied scripture, memorized verses, and then quoted truth to overcome the lies of Satan. You can do the same. Read the Bible daily and diligently. Memorize passages that will empower you to put off selfish and unholy thoughts that Satan presents to your sinful nature. Then, at the moment of enticement, recall what scripture says in relation to that temptation. Identify the tempting thought as incompatible with scripture, discard it as falsehood, and keep your focus on God's Word and will. As you imitate Christ in resisting temptation, you participate in His divine nature. You take on His attitudes, His actions, and His attributes. Subsequently, you leave behind the old ways of the sinful nature as you tap into your identity as an authentic Christian.

Resisting temptation is like changing the channel on your television. Suppose something impure from a movie, sitcom, or commercial appears on your screen. You simply and quickly flip the remote to a different channel. You choose to filter out that picture and replace it with something pure. You can do the same thing with temptation. When the devil presents an unholy thought to your fleshly nature, you filter it out. You delete that thought from your internal screen by choosing to ignore it and then change your spiritual viewing. How does this occur? You turn to the truth of God's Word! Take a moment to reflect on this illustration:

TV Screen	Mental Screen
↓	↓
Unholy Picture	Unholy Thought
↓	↓
Remote Control	Scripture Control
↓	↓
Pure Viewing	Pure Thought

I struggled as a young man with the temptation of workaholism. I attempted to do more than was humanly possible, driven by the thought that "enough was never enough." Finally, I realized this internal drivenness was different from a motivation to be an exemplary worker. I accepted the spiritual truth that the devil was behind this thought. He had planted the "enough is never enough" falsehood in my mind. It was a temptation, a lie that distracted me from closeness with God and closeness with others. As long as I bought into the lie, Satan kept me so busy that I couldn't develop healthy relationships. I came to this awareness only after I memorized these verses:

28Come to me, all you who are weary and burdened, and I will give you rest. 29Take my yoke upon you and learn from me, for I am gentle and humble in heart, and you will find rest for your souls. 30For my yoke is easy and my burden is light. (Matthew 11:28-30)

Satan continued to whisper in my spiritual ear the same temptations: "You have to do this task now ... You can't stop until you are finished ... You must get everything done today ... You need to work harder ... You have to do more, no matter how tired you are." But I would recall Matthew 11:28-30, refusing to respond out of my old nature, which only produced weariness. Instead, I responded out of my new nature, which produced restfulness. With the truth of God's Word planted deep in the rich soil of my heart, I overcame this temptation. My mental screen no longer fixated on the ruthless idea that "enough was never enough." I submitted to "scripture control" and my thoughts switched over to the purity of God's will.

I learned the life-changing lesson of rest, for Jesus never encouraged a lifestyle of heavy burdens or compulsive responsibility. Now the scripture constrained me, not the enticements of the devil. The thoughts on my internal screen were transformed by the power of God's Word. I am fully convinced that you cannot effectively resist temptation until you sufficiently know and apply scripture. Jesus said, "If you hold to my teaching, you are really my disciples. Then you will know the truth, and the truth will set you free" (John 8:31-32). I held on to the teaching of Jesus. My heart knew, without a doubt, He wanted me to experience His rest. I applied His Word whenever tempted. The result? His truth set me free from the bondage of workaholism.

A Common Error

Christians often quote Bible passages to resist temptation, as I have advocated. However, the conflict between sinfulness and godliness is not settled by merely reciting God's Word. There must be personal application of those verses to daily life. Consider the Pledge of Allegiance: *I pledge allegiance to the Flag of the United States of America, and to the Republic for which it stands, one Nation under God, indivisible, with liberty and justice for all.* It's one thing for Americans to memorize the Pledge of Allegiance and to quote it at appropriate times and places. But its application looks quite different. Do Americans respect the flag? Do they honor their country? Do they display attitudes and actions that are conducive to a united nation? Do they put their trust in God who sovereignly rules over the United States? Do they really ascribe to liberty and justice for all?

You can quickly see the huge difference between quoting words and living out the truth of those words from the heart. As a Christian, you are transformed by scripture in your heart, not just in your mouth. The devil will not be defeated by biblical quotation alone. He will be overcome by complete surrender of your heart to God's will in God's Word, for Satan holds no power over a heart yielded to the truth of scripture. This was the case with Jesus. He studied the Old Testament and obviously memorized verses. These truths were stored in His heart. When temptation came, He responded not just verbally, but spiritually. Spiritual power presided in His quotation of verses because He applied those words. He fully meant and modeled what He said. Jesus did not merely recite words. He constantly demonstrated the deep devotion of His heart to follow God's Word no matter what.

How can you follow the example of Jesus and overcome temptation? Practice the simple truths of this chapter:

1. **Be Realistic** — Accept your vulnerability. You will be tempted, for no one is immune to the enticements of the devil.
2. **Be Ready** — Memorize relevant scripture. You need the Word of God immediately available as your spiritual weapon.
3. **Be Responsible** — Refocus your thoughts. You can turn your internal screen from selfishness to godliness when tempted to travel the road of least resistance.
4. **Be Resolved** — Live God's Word. You will overcome spiritual opposition as you walk out spiritual truth.

Authentic Christianity is measured by the road chosen day in and day out. Let your choices rise from the truth of God's word, the power of which sets you free to overcome temptation and walk the path that's sometimes difficult, but always triumphant.

Application Questions
for Chapter 7 — Temptation

1. Explain the difference between temptation and sin.

2. How does temptation represent the path of least resistance?

3. What is our primary spiritual weapon against temptation? Why is it always victorious?

4. In what area of temptation do you feel most vulnerable? (Pride, materialism, deception, gossip, impatience, resentment, impurity, envy, dissension, etc.)

5. Share how a portion of scripture has empowered you to overcome a temptation and how you live differently as a result.

Chapter 8

Trials

The Road of Greatest Purpose

*"Only through experience of trial and suffering
can the soul be strengthened, vision cleared,
ambition inspired, and success achieved."*
Helen Keller

Trials are Inevitable

Trials, in the scripture, mean any difficulty, hardship or adversity that challenges spiritual maturity. As it is with temptation, so it is with trials — you are not exempt! I fully came to this conclusion, personally and dramatically, on January 15, 1980. Awakened in the middle of the night by a loud, crashing noise, I jumped out of bed and found my wife had fallen in the adjacent bathroom. I had no idea what was wrong and was unable to bring Bev to consciousness. All I could do was move her out of the small bathroom to the floor of our bedroom.

I quickly called an ambulance and then our doctor. The ten-minute wait seemed like an eternity. Once the paramedics arrived and gently carried Bev to the ambulance, I drove to the hospital where our doctor was ready to begin tests. Soon he discovered Bev was pregnant. However, the egg had lodged in a curved part of the fallopian tube. As a result, the baby could not develop properly. This led to the rupture of the fallopian tube and a huge amount of internal bleeding. Emergency surgery and four pints of blood transfusions saved Bev's life.

This ectopic pregnancy emotionally jolted us into both shock and pain. It was shocking because we didn't know Bev was pregnant. It was painful because we lost a baby. In addition, the surgeon told us that the other fallopian tube also curved considerably. Therefore, we faced the high probability we would never have children. My wife endured 12 weeks of physical recuperation following the surgery, but most disheartening was the trauma of losing a baby. We grieved our loss for many months.

Before this time of shock and pain, I didn't realize life could be so cruel. I felt invulnerable. Subconsciously, I believed bad things didn't happen to good people, especially Christians. But I was wrong. No one stands exempt from trials. Fortunately, God's grace and mercy are greater than the agony of any hardship. In our case, Christian friends surrounded us with comfort. More significantly, God held us in His arms of love as we cried, prayed, and worshipped. We not only survived, we matured through our trial. (And the Lord later blessed us with three wonderful children!)

Trials are Purposeful

The Bible says:

> [2]*Consider it pure joy, my brothers, whenever you face trials of many kinds,* [3]*because you know that the testing of your faith develops perseverance.* [4]*Perseverance must finish its work so that you may be mature and complete, not lacking anything.* [5]*If any of you lacks wisdom, he should ask God, who gives generously to all without finding fault, and it will be given to him. (James 1:2-5)*

Notice, in verses 3 and 4, that trials test your faith for the purpose of maturity. This doesn't mean God sends hardship your way just so you can "grow up." Rather, you encounter difficulties because you are an imperfect person, living in an imperfect body, with an imperfect mind, in an imperfect world, alongside other imperfect people! Like everyone else on the planet, you are bound to experience tough times.

The promise from this passage provides encouragement for these tough times. Suffering is not meaningless. Adversity is not without hope. God makes good come out of bad. Difficulties, then, do not portray enemies, but servants. Your problems serve you by giving occasion for personal growth. They supply opportunities for spiritual trust to rise higher and spiritual character to grow deeper. In this sense, trials build the road of greatest purpose, maturing you into the likeness of Jesus Christ.

My friend, Ron, discovered this truth after a terrible auto accident. As a young doctor, he worked at a hospital in central Pennsylvania. He traveled narrow, winding roads through the countryside to see his hospitalized patients. One day, in snowy weather, Ron lost control of his sports car. His vehicle flew off the side of the road and slammed into a ditch, where it was invisible to other motorists. Hours later, Ron was found, removed from the car and transported to the hospital. There he endured hours of surgery, including amputation of one of his legs.

Ron eventually recovered his strength and resumed his career. He does not harbor resentment toward God for "letting this happen." Rather, he rejoices because he survived physically and matured spiritually. Ron learned to persevere, becoming more like Jesus who learned "obedience from what He suffered" (Hebrews 5:8).

My friend knew suffering is a common part of life. He observed it daily in his medical practice long before his own pain and hardship. Now, as a doctor who rides the halls of the hospital in a motorized wheelchair to check on patients, Ron lives through adversity. He will tell you that God did not plan this trial, but it came nonetheless. He doesn't try to figure it out. Instead, Ron holds fast to the purpose of spiritual maturity that God graciously provides in any circumstance that challenges our faith.

Returning to James 1:3, the Greek word used for "testing" designated approval. This word, *dokimos*, is found by archeologists on the underside of many pieces of pottery in the Near East. The marking of *dokimos* meant the piece persevered through the fire of the kiln without cracking. It was approved. It passed the test of perseverance!

The same is true for you. God's redemptive desire, through fiery trials, is to form you into a tempered and unbreakable clay vessel. The word "complete" (vs. 4) summarizes the result of testing. You are made more complete, more like Jesus, when you persevere through the intense heat of troubling times and challenging circumstances. Unavoidable trials can cause unparalleled maturity.

Therefore, do not be discouraged by trials and question God's goodness. Instead, be transformed by trials and rejoice in God's goodness. "Consider it pure joy" when trials come (vs. 2). Don't rejoice in the problem or the suffering, but in the opportunity to become more Christ-like. This is what Ron did, profoundly passing the test of his trial. Ron epitomizes authentic Christianity, starting strong and staying strong regardless of adversity.

While rejoicing in the occasion to mature, you need wisdom to forge through turbulent moments. This is why James says, "If any of you lacks wisdom, he should ask God, who gives generously" (vs. 5). Often Christians inquire of God, "Why did you let this happen to me?" This question demands an explanation from God, and possibly justification, so as to understand the reason for a trial. However, you don't need to know (and many times won't know) why certain things happen to you. Knowing "why" does not necessarily solve your problems, anyway. There is only one path through your trials and that is straight through your trials.

Wisdom from God does not consist in understanding why you go through a difficulty. Rather, it is a matter of knowing how to persevere through a difficulty. So, ask God for wisdom. Ask Him to show you what to do. Ask Him to remind you of scriptures to encourage you. Ask Him to renew your perspective. Ask Him to direct you to trustworthy people for counsel. Ask Him to make you more complete like Jesus Christ. Knowing why you've encountered a trial may possibly be helpful, but knowing how to respond in a trial is absolutely essential. By majoring on "how" instead of "why," you are poised to learn perseverance that leads to maturity. It's the road of greatest purpose in times of trouble.

Trials are Unpredictable

Trials can come to you in "many kinds" (vs. 2). The kinds of adversity experienced over a lifetime may vary greatly, such as unemployment, loss of a loved one, injury, sickness, breakdown of a friendship, indebtedness, divorce, etc.

Furthermore, you can't forecast when problems might arise. For example, many years ago I was blindsided by the onset of a chemical imbalance in my brain. I didn't understand it. I only knew "my brain was sick." I struggled and prayed for 13 years, trying to overcome this illness. Finally, I found a doctor who prescribed medication that restored my mental equilibrium within two months of treatment. What a relief from a long-term sickness that was totally unexpected!

Hardships are extremely unpredictable. They present themselves in various shapes and sizes. They show up when you don't anticipate their arrival. They appear one at a time or seemingly all at once. Remember the good news, though. These trials are your servants. They test your faith, develop your perseverance, and mature your character. Therefore, consider it pure joy whenever you face trials! They may be humanly unpredictable, but they are divinely purposeful.

Take a look at the following acrostic using the word TRIAL. It contains five practical ways to apply this chapter. Put these into practice, and you will know the purpose of maturity whenever you face trials of many kinds.

T — Trust God

> [8]*We do not want you to be uninformed, brothers, about the hardships we suffered in the province of Asia. We were under great pressure, far beyond our ability to endure, so that we despaired even of life.* [9]*Indeed, in our hearts we felt the sentence of death. But this happened that we might not rely on ourselves but on God, who raises the dead. (2 Corinthians 1:8-9)*

The apostle Paul authored this passage. He worked diligently in the first-century church as a leader, teacher, pastor, and missionary. Paul withstood an unimaginable series of hardships during the course of his ministry. He was beaten, shipwrecked, betrayed, and imprisoned. The weight of these ongoing pressures nearly immobilized Paul. However, he repeatedly placed his trust in the Lord, avoiding hopelessness and despair. What an example of authentic Christianity!

My chemical imbalance pales in comparison to the sufferings of the apostle Paul. Nevertheless, I understand the reality of a deflated, discouraged heart. My brain sickness produced melancholy thoughts, emotional upheaval, and constant fatigue. I tried so hard, but never could figure out why I felt so bad. While worshipping one Sunday morning I said to the Lord, "I can't take anymore. You have to heal me now." I did not find healing for my illness that day, but I did receive healing for my heart. I learned to trust. I stopped making demands on God, and I stopped relying on myself. Long before a medical answer was found, I uncovered the invaluable lesson of trusting God to sustain me in my trial. He raised Jesus from the dead, so surely He could carry me through this suffering. He did, and I'm so glad that He is trustworthy.

R —   Receive care

Carry each other's burdens, and in this way you will fulfill the law of Christ. (Galatians 6:2)

A common temptation during trials is to withdraw from fellow Christians. This may occur because of embarrassment, afraid of others knowing how weak you really are. It may also happen because of unrealistic expectation, trying to prove how strong you'd like to be. However, Galatians 6:2 says we need each other. In fact, carrying each other's burdens displays a normal part of Christian life, a common way to fulfill the law of Christ, which is the law of love.

I benefited from the compassion of fellow Christians throughout the painful years of my chemical imbalance. In particular, I asked a few close friends to pray for me every week for an hour. They gathered around me with support and encouragement that proved life-changing. I eagerly anticipated each prayer time together, assured of a fresh dose of God's love in and through my Christian friends. Their caring gave me strength to never give up. Therefore, don't isolate yourself when you experience a trial. Stay close to other believers in fellowship, worship, prayer and dialogue. Then you can receive the love of God necessary to forge through any trial.

You might ask, "How do I find the care I need?" Well, if you are new to a church home, call the church office. Tell them you are facing a difficult situation and need someone with whom you can speak. If you have a church home, talk with Christian friends in the fellowship. You could confide with someone in your Sunday School class, a person in your small group, or your small group leader. In an emergency, of course, you should call one of the pastors as well.

I — Ignore Satan

… For the accuser of our brothers, who accuses them before our God day and night, has been hurled down. (Revelation 12:10)

Satan, the devil, is described here as the accuser. He loves to harass Christians. So, he attempts to take advantage of your trials by using them as opportunity to put you down. He may whisper accusations in your spiritual ear such as: "You are so stupid … You'll never make it through this … You might as well give up." The concept of Satan, the spiritual enemy of Christians, may be new or seem strange to some. The Bible, though, is crystal-clear about the devil. Scripture calls him the "father of lies" (John 8:44). He works to defeat followers of Christ by misleading them with false messages, especially during adversity.

For example, my illness depleted most of my energy. Periodically, I could do nothing but rest. At other times, I mustered enough energy to do some of my pastoral ministry. The devil, however, tried to convince me that I couldn't do anything at all. Therefore, I had to ignore Satan's lies when he said, "Your ministry is over ... You can't do anything ... Look at how tired you are ... You might as well sit at home the rest of your life." Gradually, I perceived these statements as false accusations spoken by the father of lies. I learned to ignore them as falsehood. Then, I would remind myself of the truth that my ministry was not over, that I could do whatever God gives me strength to do, and I could even do things when fatigued. What freedom I found sorting through the messages in my mind, sifting out lies and laying hold of truth.

This process correlates with the way you resist temptation, as explained in the previous chapter. Truth, especially the truth of scripture, forms your spiritual weapon to deflect and disarm the false messages of Satan. One day Satan will be hurled down into the abyss of hell. Until then, you must ignore his schemes to capitalize on your difficulties. He only wants to discourage you in the midst of your trials and distract you from the purpose behind your trials. Therefore, resist the devil by refusing to listen to his blaming and condemning voice.

A —   **Accept yourself**

> *… Christ accepted you … (Romans 15:7)*

Jesus accepted you perfectly and completely. Now you can apply this same sense of acceptance to yourself. There isn't a more significant time for self-acceptance than during a trial, for it's just too easy to get down on yourself when life turns sour.

To illustrate, a friend of mine endured an illness similar to mine, one caused by a chemical imbalance. I'll never forget talking with her in the church parking lot after a meeting. I told her how awful I felt lately. I also shared how guilty I felt for feeling so terrible. My friend looked me straight in the eye and said, "It's not your fault!" Suddenly, shame started to drain out of me and grace began to fill me up. It was one of those rare "aha" experiences. Freedom flooded my soul as I seized the Christ-like acceptance my friend offered. That day shame met defeat. No longer would I criticize myself for having an illness. Instead, I would view myself as a perfectly loved and completely accepted human being.

Treat yourself, then, as Jesus has and always will. Accept yourself right where you are — your humanness, vulnerability, weakness — regardless of the trial you encounter. Ignore Satan's accusations, and also ignore self-criticism. This application of God's grace in tough times will free you to see beyond your trial and keep a godly perspective during your trial. Accept yourself.

L — Leave bitterness

Get rid of all bitterness, rage and anger, brawling and slander, along with every form of malice. (Ephesians 4:31)

Trials make you better or bitter. You get to choose. It's okay to feel angry about your trials, but it's not okay to stay angry and become bitter.

This chapter commenced with the story of my wife's near-fatal ectopic pregnancy, which created huge emotional turmoil. As for me, I explored depths of anger I didn't know existed. Maybe I could identify reasons for my anger like the shock of the circumstances, the uncertainty of Bev surviving emergency surgery, and the high probability we would never have children. Regardless of understanding the reasons for my anger, it was present, profound, and powerful. How would I deal with this emotion that nearly overwhelmed me?

First, I expressed my feelings to God more than once! He is strong and loving enough to accept emotional honesty. Secondly, I prayed that my attitude would not color any relationship, with God or others, in a negative way. Third, I reminded myself of scripture such as: "In your anger do not sin ..." (Ephesians 4:26). The Bible comforted me with the freedom to be angry and articulate my emotion before God. It also directed me to avoid a sinful attitude of bitterness. I'm glad I got better, not bitter.

I wish we all lived in the garden of Eden, the perfect world God created. But, we don't! The actions of Adam and Eve recorded in Genesis, the first book of the Bible, left us with an imperfect world wherein trials are commonplace. We can blame Adam and Eve, ourselves, others, or even God, when trials knock on our door. But my invitation to you is to become better, not bitter. Leave bitterness by acknowledging the inevitability and unpredictability of trials. Then embrace God's redeeming love which turns bad into good, pain into joy, unrest into peace. Remember the road of greatest purpose when you go through tough times: Your Heavenly Father will even use trials to make you more complete, like Jesus.

Application Questions
for Chapter 8 — Trials

1. What purpose lies within our trials?

2. Why are we told to pray for wisdom during hard times?

3. How does Satan often tempt us as we go through difficulties?

4. How do we distinguish between God's voice and the lies of Satan? What lie has the devil presented to you, but you identified and rebuked it? Do you need further help in this area?

5. Share a trial you encountered in the past couple years. How did you endure? What did you learn about trusting God? What would you do differently if you faced a similar trial in the future?

Chapter 9

Ministry

Sharing the Love of Christ

*"... the Son of Man did not come to be served,
but to serve ..." Jesus (Matthew 20:28)*

The more you become like Jesus, the more you'll share His love with others. Your heart will expand in its desire to serve like Christ, who continually gave Himself away. Jesus welcomed strangers, fed the hungry, taught the multitudes, confronted religious hypocrites, prayed for the sick, and blessed little children. Compassionate ministry characterized the life of Christ. The Lord's example invited and equipped His original followers to join Him in a lifetime of service. The same is true today. You are called to serve, demonstrating the love of Christ. Ministry, sharing the love of Christ, happens in three ways: using natural talents, implementing spiritual gifts, and doing good deeds.

Natural Talents

Talents are God-given abilities, inherent in how He created you. You may possess a musical, athletic, intellectual, domestic, mechanical, or artistic talent. Take inventory and identify what the Lord deposited in you. Why? Because God wants you to nurture your talents, developing the abilities He has entrusted to you. In addition, He delights in the discovery of times and places to use your talents, giving away what He invested in you. Natural talents are not merely areas in which you excel. These God-given abilities reveal His blessing, creativity, and purpose. Talents enable you to honor God as you serve others.

Dorcas provides an outstanding example. She utilized her domestic talent of making clothes to help the needy. Dorcas was "always doing good and helping the poor" (Acts 9:36). She recognized and dedicated her God-given ability to bless not just her own family, but many others. Like Dorcas, assess, develop, and apply your talents. God will be faithful to bless your ministry as you are faithful to bless others.

Unlike Dorcas, I received no domestic talents. However, God gave me athletic talent. I didn't realize, until many years after becoming a Christian, how this talent could be a means for ministry. Let me explain. I attended a graduate school in southern California in the late '70s. My wife worked full-time, but we needed more money for living expenses and my tuition. So, I applied for a part-time position on the staff of a Japanese-American church. (Ethnic churches were not unusual in that part of the nation.)

To my surprise and delight, the church leaders extended an offer which I accepted. I experienced deep joy building relationships with these kind and gentle people. At the same time, I was startled by the fact that many of them had a family history of Buddhism. Consequently, a percentage of the congregation did not enjoy a genuine relationship with Jesus, although they were quite involved in the church.

Tennis was a very popular sport with numerous young adults in this fellowship. I also enjoyed tennis and was often invited to play doubles. I soon gained credibility as a good tennis player, which set the stage for something far more important. My Japanese-American friends started watching me closely. As they observed my talent, they formed a positive impression of me. It was not long until they began asking questions about my faith in Jesus.

Subsequently, I had the privilege to lead an entire family into personal relationship with Jesus as Savior and Lord. Soon, others devoted themselves to Christ as well. I wonder if this life-transforming ministry would have ever happened if I was not blessed with the athletic talent of tennis. I doubt it. Without me even knowing it, God used my talent as a context for developing relationship and a stage for performing ministry.

I am extremely proud of our children and how they deploy their natural talents in ministry. For example, God graced our oldest child, Bethany, with extraordinary passion for and proficiency in foreign languages. She began the study of French in eighth grade, completing five years of study by the time she graduated from high school. She continued her studies at Baylor University and majored in Language & Linguistics, which included French, Italian, and Chinese.

One day when I was visiting Bethany on campus, she insisted on stopping by the university's bookstore. I didn't let on, but I knew what she wanted. She wanted me to buy her a new sweatshirt or some other piece of Baylor apparel. Right? Wrong! We walked swiftly past all the clothing racks to a back corner of the store. There we stood, surrounded by shelves and shelves of foreign language books. Then Bethany exclaimed, "I want to learn all of these!" I'll never forget that moment. She identified, beyond a shadow of a doubt, her God-given talent. She also evidenced a devotion to be faithful with that talent.

In 2004 and 2005, Bethany taught English to students in France. She worked alongside American missionaries in her free time, instructing immigrants to France how to read and write the French language. Bethany discovered these two outlets for her God-given abilities right after college graduation. What amazing opportunities to help others and honor God!

Consider your natural talents. What has God given you? What if, right now, you put into practice the talents you have? Those to whom you minister

— family, friends, church, coworkers, classmates, neighbors — will be tremendously blessed. Don't wait to use your talents! Like Jesus, let your life be characterized by ministry.

Spiritual Gifts

Your ministry also includes spiritual gifts. Gifts are God-given like natural talents. However, they are not inherent in who God made you as a human being. Rather, they consist of supernatural abilities that God gives once you become a Christian. All people possess talents, but only Christians receive spiritual gifts. The following biblical passages emphasize these gifts.

⁶We have different gifts, according to the grace given us. If a man's gift is prophesying, let him use it in proportion to his faith. ⁷If it is serving, let him serve; if it is teaching, let him teach; ⁸if it is encouraging, let him encourage; if it is contributing to the needs of others, let him give generously; if it is leadership, let him govern diligently; if it is showing mercy, let him do it cheerfully. (Romans 12:6-8)

¹Now about spiritual gifts, brothers, I do not want you to be ignorant. … ⁴There are different kinds of gifts, but the same Spirit. ⁵There are different kinds of service, but the same Lord. ⁶There are different kinds of working, but the same God works all of them in all men.

[7]Now to each one the manifestation of the Spirit is given for the common good. [8]To one there is given through the Spirit the message of wisdom, to another the message of knowledge by means of the same Spirit, [9]to another faith by the same Spirit, to another gifts of healing by that one Spirit, [10]to another miraculous powers, to another prophecy, to another distinguishing between spirits, to another speaking in different kinds of tongues, and to still another the interpretation of tongues. [11]All these are the work of one and the same Spirit, and he gives them to each one, just as he determines. (1 Corinthians 12:1-11)

[11]It was he who gave some to be apostles, some to be prophets, some to be evangelists, and some to be pastors and teachers, [12]to prepare God's people for works of service, so that the body of Christ may be built up ... (Ephesians 4:11-12).

[9]Offer hospitality to one another without grumbling. [10]Each one should use whatever gift he has received to serve others, faithfully administering God's grace in its various forms. [11]If anyone speaks, he should do it as one speaking the very words of God. If anyone serves, he should do it with the strength God provides, so that in all things God may be praised through Jesus Christ. To him be the glory and the power for ever and ever. Amen. (1 Peter 4:9-11)

You can readily see the numerous and diverse gifts available to followers of Christ. Along with natural talents, spiritual gifts comprise the primary tools to accomplish the ministry purposes God planned for you. Look at the gifts mentioned in Romans 12:8 (the first scripture passage). God will give you the gift of encouragement if He wants you to spur others forward, on a consistent basis, with words of kindness. He will impart the gift of giving to you if His will involves regularly assisting others financially. The Lord will grant you the gift of leadership if His purpose entails supervision of others in ministry. And God will bestow the gift of mercy if He chooses to display His empathy and compassion through you in a recurring fashion.

You need not qualify, or meet a certain set of requirements, in order to receive spiritual gifts. A college education is not necessary to have the spiritual gift of teaching. An extroverted personality is not necessary to have the gift of leadership. A high IQ is not necessary to have the gift of knowledge or wisdom. God sovereignly determines your gifts in harmony with the plans He designed for you. Therefore, trust that the supernatural abilities you receive are always best for you and your ministry of sharing the love of Christ.

Although prerequisites for spiritual gifts do not exist, let me offer some noteworthy guidelines for distinguishing and deploying your gifts:

1. Individual Prayer — 1 Corinthians 14:1 — "Eagerly desire spiritual gifts."

God personally invites you to ask for gifts so you can know Him better and sense His heartbeat for ministry. After all, He is the giver of spiritual gifts and the initiator of ministry. Through these times of prayer, your spirit and will aligns with God's Spirit and will, whether or not you receive the gift(s) requested.

For example, I've often prayed for the gift of healing. However, I haven't been graced with that gift. Instead, the Lord entrusted to me the gifts of leadership, teaching, and encouragement. I certainly pray for those who are ill. However, I spend little time praying for sick people compared to the time I spend studying for upcoming teachings. I accept my gifts and ministry, and major on the obvious course carved out for me. My spirit and will rest content with the knowledge that I eagerly desire spiritual gifts and with the assurance my God-given gifts match my God-given ministry.

2. Gifts Workshop — 1 Corinthians 12:27 — "Now you are the body of Christ, and each one of you is a part of it."

Many churches offer workshops, seminars, or conferences to assist people in the process of identifying spiritual gifts. Although these courses should not replace prayer, the questionnaires and inventories employed at these workshops can benefit you greatly. They indicate a high probability of gifting in one or more areas of ministry. Pray and talk with others about the results. Make sure to pay close attention to the direction gained at a spiritual gifts workshop. And remember that you are a unique part of the body of Christ, the church. The Lord has special plans reserved for you.

3. **Small Group** — Proverbs 27:17 — "As iron sharpens iron, so one man sharpens another."

The best place to begin exercising spiritual gifts is usually in a fellowship group or other small group. First, your fellow Christians furnish a safe environment. You can experiment with how and when to use your gifts without fear of criticism. In addition, the effectiveness of your spiritual gifts can be sharpened. Others in your group can encourage and counsel you in the continued development and maximum impact of your gifts.

I remember how my first small group graciously allowed me to teach. I tried my best, despite very limited Bible knowledge. My messages fell far below any standard of excellence. However, the group cared more about me than my gift. Therefore, they listened closely, affirmed me, and let me teach again! Further opportunities motivated me to study diligently and nurtured my gift of conveying God's Word in a relevant and practical manner. I wouldn't be teaching a church of 800 today if I didn't start experimenting with this gift in a group of eight. Let your small group sharpen your ministry!

4. **Pastoral Leaders** — Hebrews 13:17 — "Obey your leaders and submit to their authority. They keep watch over you as men who must give an account ..."

God designed His church with spiritual leaders to nurture its health and oversee its maturity. This includes the well-being and growth of your ministry. Therefore, discuss ministry opportunities with small group leaders and other pastoral leaders of your church. Solicit feedback as you begin using spiritual gifts. Submit to pastoral authority. The leaders in your fellowship can help you find a ministry niche where you can be most effective.

5. **Divine Love** — 1 Corinthians 13:2 — "If I have the gift of prophecy and can fathom all mysteries and all knowledge, and if I have a faith that can move mountains, but have not love, I am nothing."

The gift of prophecy, knowledge, faith, or any other gift, is mere action apart from God's love. The implementation of spiritual gifts warrants compassion because the over-riding purpose is ministry! Without heartfelt concern, gifts lack substance. In fact, they may be utilized for selfish reasons, such as gaining favor or personal attention. Gifts might even be used to "fix" someone's problem rather than care for someone's heart. In the absence of love, ministry is empty and selfish. Therefore, pray not only for the power of spiritual gifts, but also for the motivation of divine love. Gifts coupled with love majorly depict authentic Christianity.

Good Deeds

Good deeds differ from both natural talents and spiritual gifts. They encompass acts of service that need to be done in everyday life, i.e., meeting basic needs, listening to a friend's concern, visiting someone who is sick, complimenting a co-worker for a job well done, offering a neighbor assistance with his project, or affirming your love for your family. Countless avenues, which don't require a talent or gift, abound for serving Jesus with good deeds. Let me share four directives to help you capitalize on these opportunities:

1. Start where you are.

Numerous serving possibilities surround you. Just look at the people with whom you have regular contact. Ask yourself about each one, "How could I share Christ's love with this person through a good deed?"

Jesus set a monumental example when He washed the feet of His disciples (John 13:1-17). In the midst of sharing a meal together, Christ got up, wrapped a towel around His waist, poured water into a basin, and began to clean the dirty feet of His followers. This task belonged to a household slave who washed the feet of guests. Apparently no servant was available when the Lord and His men arrived. Therefore,

Jesus assumed the position of a slave as He knelt to remove the dirt and dust from their feet.

When Jesus completed this humble act of service, He told His disciples, "I have set you an example that you should do as I have done for you" (John 13:15). What could you do to emulate the model of Jesus? Whom could you serve? When? Where? Take inventory of your relationships, and let good deeds start where you are.

2. Use what you have.

The deliverance of Israel from slavery in Egypt is one of the great Bible stories. It begins with God telling Moses to lead the Hebrew nation out from underneath the oppressive rule of Pharoah. Moses, however, questioned his ability to serve God in this way. He perceived himself as inadequate, saying, "Who am I, that I should go to Pharoah and bring the Israelites out of Egypt?" (Exodus 3:11). Although God promised His presence and power, Moses struggled to accept the task. He said, "What if they [Pharoah and the Egyptians] do not believe me or listen to me …?" (Exodus 4:1).

In addition, Moses doubted his ability to speak clearly enough for the job required. Finally, he blurted out his deep-seated reluctance, "O Lord, please send someone else to do it" (Exodus 4:13). But the Lord said to him, "What is that in your hand?" "A staff," he replied (Exodus 4:2). Moses used that staff to tend sheep for 40 years. He didn't have much, but he did have a staff. In other words, God wasn't taking "no" for an answer. God expected Moses to use what he had and serve as His representative.

Therefore, the Lord directed Moses to lead the Hebrews out of bondage and into freedom with that singular resource, the shepherd's staff. And so he did! Moses performed miracles with that one thing he had. He even parted the Red Sea by raising his staff over the water. As a result, the Israelites escaped Egypt, crossing the sea on dry ground.

You might experience reservations similar to those of Moses. Certainly your good deeds are of less significance historically. Nevertheless, your sense of awkwardness, reluctance, or insecurity may be equally strong. You might wish God would send someone else to do what He instructs only you to fulfill. So, remember the good news that God has placed something in your hand. By His grace you have what is needed to complete what is required. Look at your hand. What is in your grasp? Hold fast to it for God. You can do many good deeds if you just use what you have!

3. Do what is necessary.

Most deeds of kindness revolve around the daily responsibilities of providing for family, showing concern for friends, and giving the best effort on the job. However, opportunities to serve come in a wide variety. For example, our church held a work day some years ago. We planned to clean up the outside of our property by raking leaves, mowing grass, washing off the parking lot, and trimming trees.

I needed to cut my own lawn and trim my own trees that particular Saturday. At the same time, I knew the church grounds required a lot of work and somebody needed to step up as an example. Therefore, I left my own yard work undone and went to serve the church. I recall trimming every tree on the 3 acres. My lawn and trees still demanded attention when I returned home, but I was too tired. Nevertheless, I knew in my heart I did the right thing, esteeming the basic needs of the church above my own.

I wish I could claim to be servant-oriented on a continual basis. However, I do know a man who has been a consistent model of good deeds throughout his life. His name is Jim Garrett. Jim was the first pastor with whom I worked in a church setting. I joined this 20-year veteran of pastoral ministry at a small church in Tulsa, Oklahoma in 1976.

Newly married, my wife and I moved to Tulsa the day before I started alongside Jim as the Associate Pastor. We were so excited about this new ministry that we decided to drive by the church building late that night. We passed by and noticed a light on in the church offices. We pulled in the parking lot and recognized Jim's car. Wondering what he was doing in the office so late at night, we walked in the door, down the hallway, and into the office area. We couldn't believe our eyes. There was Jim, the Senior Pastor for 20 years, finishing the construction of my new office. He had chosen to stay all night, if needed, to complete the office for my initial day on the job. This act of kindness will never fade from my memory.

My dad told me when I was a kid, "There are times you need to do things that just need to be done." Honestly, I rebelled against that counsel when I was a teenager. I wanted to do only what I wanted to do! Later I comprehended the truth that ministry is often a simple act of service, doing what it takes to bless someone else, doing things that just need to be done. These good deeds reflect authentic Christianity.

4. Find what is next.

Once you start where you are, use what you have, and do what is necessary, you will be in optimal position to find what is next for you in ministry. In other words, as you prove yourself faithful with the more obvious responsibilities to serve, God will reveal to you more opportunities. Jesus said, "You have been faithful with a few things; I will put you in charge of many things ..." (Matthew 25:21). God rewards you with further dimensions of ministry as you intentionally and habitually carry out the good deeds of everyday life.

The biblical characters of Stephen and Philip clearly illustrate this truth. Both were chosen as deacons in the early church to oversee the daily distribution of food to poor widows (Acts 6:1-6). They faithfully served by managing the food supplies. Consequently, God increased the scope of their ministries. Stephen "did great wonders and miraculous signs among the people" (Acts 6:8). Philip received the ministry of an evangelist and also performed miraculous signs and healings through the power of the Holy Spirit (Acts 8:5-40).

How did Stephen and Philip find what was next in God's plans for their ministries? They started right where they were, willing to accept an administrative task. Then they used what they had, wisdom to develop a plan of food distribution. Then they did what was necessary, daily supervising this ministry to the poor. Then God opened more doors for them to proclaim and demonstrate the good news of Jesus Christ.

A friend of mine in college once said to me, "The more you do what you know, the more you know what to do." I've realized the profound nature of this principle time and time again. So, allow me to encourage you. Do what you know to serve Christ, and like Stephen and Philip, you'll find what is next.

5. Serve on a team.

The New Testament church prioritized team ministry wherein mutual support, prayer, and accountability took place. Teammates also complemented one another's gifts, talents, and service. This unity maximized the influence of the early church, dramatically re-shaping the spiritual landscape of their society.

Ideally, you will serve on a ministry team(s) whereby similar harmony and impact take place. Team members working side by side (as in business or athletics) create wider vision, generate more energy, carry greater responsibility, and execute deeper change. Implementing talents, spiritual gifts, and good deeds merely on an individual basis will not achieve God's overall design for the church or society.

Interestingly, nature provides various parallels to the principle of spiritual teamwork. For example, I helped one of my children many years ago with a school project about bees, specifically worker bees. I learned that each bee maintains a specific responsibility. Some build rooms in the beehive. Others care for the baby bees. A segment assist the queen bee. Still others guard the hive, chasing away wasps and various insects that attempt to steal the honey. Some bees fly out from the beehive to collect pollen and nectar from flowers. Finally, a contingent of worker bees stays at the beehive door, flapping their wings speedily to blow cool air through the hive.

Worker bees paint a model picture of serving as a team in a comprehensive and effective manner. Make sure you don't stand alone, then, in your spiritual work. Serving alongside others promotes a lot of fun and friendship. More importantly, teamwork thoroughly and successfully accomplishes the will of God.

Application Questions
for Chapter 9 — Ministry

Natural Talents

1. Name your natural talents.

2. How have your talents built relationship with people or served others? In the church? Elsewhere?

Spiritual Gifts

1. What spiritual gifts has God given you?

2. Which one is most obvious? Give an example of how you serve others with this gift?

3. If you have not yet identified your spiritual gifts, what gift(s) would you like God to give you? In what area of service are you most eager to be involved?

4. Share what would be most beneficial in learning more about spiritual gifts and identifying your gifts. Possible examples include:

a. Praying for particular spiritual gifts.
b. Attending a spiritual gifts workshop.
c. Discussing spiritual gifts with a Christian friend or pastoral leader.
d. Asking God for ministry opportunities.
e. Studying biblical passages about spiritual gifts.
f. Participating on a ministry team within your church.

Good Deeds

1. What good deeds might you do for a family member, co-worker, friend, neighbor, fellow-student, etc.?

2. Tell of a time you served someone with a good deed and describe his/her response — good or bad.

3. Tell of a time you benefited from someone's good deed and how it made a difference in your life.

Chapter 10

Finances

Giving the Blessings of Christ

"Money is a terrible master but an excellent servant." P.T. Barnum

Ministry is essentially sharing what God has entrusted to you. As observed in Chapter 9, this involves natural talents, spiritual gifts, and good deeds. In addition, ministry includes giving of your material resources. When you turn your life over to God through repentance, the ownership of all money and possessions transfers to Him as well. You belong to God. So, naturally, He owns everything you have. You simply manage the material blessings He has graciously bestowed. In this chapter you will learn how to be a faithful manager of money by examining five questions about financial giving: Why? What? Where? When? How?

WHY

Reasons abound for giving money to the Lord. First, giving increasingly transforms you into His image. God gave everything for you when He sacrificed Jesus, His only Son. You become more like your generous God whenever sacrificing something for His sake.

Also, giving keeps your heart in proper relationship with God. Jesus said, "For where your treasure is, there your heart will be also" (Matthew 6:21). The use of money directly reflects the condition of your heart. Look at your checkbook and credit cards and you can quickly monitor your spiritual health. If you are a generous person, you have a godly heart. If you are a greedy person, you have an ungodly heart. Don't feel condemned, though, if you have been greedy. Today you can make a new beginning by transferring ownership of your resources to God, and learning how (in this chapter) to offer material blessings back to Him.

Third, giving reminds you that God is the source of all blessing. His grace supplies 100 percent of what you have, for "the earth is the Lord's, and everything in it ..." (Psalms 24:1). God owns all things. He is the Source of your money and possessions. Therefore, financial giving is actually presenting the blessings of Christ back to the One who granted them to you. Each act of giving, then, calls to mind that the Lord is your provider.

Giving also teaches you how to trust God. You may have confidence that your house, car, or insurance payment will be paid this month. Maybe you even trust that your credit card bill will be paid down or paid off. But do you believe God will take care of you if you give a portion of your income to Him? God says, "… Test me in this … and see if I will not throw open the floodgates of heaven and pour out so much blessing that you will not have room enough for it" (Malachi 3:10). The Lord challenges you to trust Him. Freely give back what He so lovingly has granted, and watch how He meets your needs.

In addition, giving tames the power of money. Money represents a power which stands in direct opposition to God. It yearns to control your life. Jesus said, "No one can serve two masters. Either he will hate the one and love the other, or he will be devoted to the one and despise the other. You cannot serve both God and Money" (Matthew 6:24). You serve only one master, either the Almighty Lord or the "almighty" dollar. The way you remain free from the power of money is to manage it and not let it manage you. Giving actualizes the first step to healthy money management, because giving away money empties it of its power. As a result, money acts as your servant instead of your master.

I periodically look back on a personal temptation related to the power of money. It occurred in 1985 while I was watching a football game on a black and white television in our family room. I started thinking about the upcoming NFL playoffs and Super Bowl. What a great time to purchase a color TV! And why not? After all, every friend of mine owned a color television. Plus, how could I appreciate the playoffs without one? Quickly, I came up with a plan. I'd simply take the $300 set aside for giving to God that month and buy a new television. This wouldn't develop into a habit, of course. I'd withhold my giving this one time and no more. God surely wouldn't mind if I acquired something everyone had but me!

Fortunately, I realized my selfish thoughts and shook off the temptation. The power of money pushed hard to get the best of me that day. It wanted to place its foot in the door of my mind, but I refused its entry by God's truth. Although I didn't get a color television for some time, I was blessed because money remained my servant, not my master. As usual, I gladly gave that $300 to the Lord, giving the blessings of Christ back to Him.

Another cause for giving is preparation to handle the spiritual riches of ministry. Jesus said, "So if you have not been trustworthy in handling worldly wealth, who will trust you with true riches?" (Luke 16:11). The Lord Himself issued a requirement for anyone who wants to work in the spiritual riches of ministry: Prove yourself faithful with money, then you are qualified to prove yourself faithful with ministry. As mentioned above, the way you manage finances reveals the condition of your heart. Therefore, if your spirit is not right, God will not allow you to handle spiritual things. Conversely, be faithful with material resources and God will release you to be faithful with the riches of His ministry in and through the church.

A final rationale for giving concerns the building of investments in heaven. Jesus said, "Do not store up for yourselves treasures on earth, where moth and rust destroy, and where thieves break in and steal. But store up for yourselves treasures in heaven, where moth and rust do not destroy, and where thieves do not break in and steal" (Matthew 6:19-20). Everything on earth will eventually wear out or be taken away, except giving! When you give to the Lord, you invest in people and ministries that will last, that which is of eternal value.

These eternal investments will be rewarded in heaven. All actions, good or bad, will be called into account "for we will all stand before God's judgment seat" (Romans 14:10), "... each of us will give an account of himself to God" (Romans 14:12), "... each will be rewarded according to his own labor" (1 Corinthians 3:8), "because you know that the Lord will reward everyone for whatever good he does ..." (Ephesians 6:8). Giving multiplies back to you in heaven, to enjoy the eternal dividends of all your earthly investments that honored the Lord.

On a visit to see our daughter at Baylor University, we heard the president of the school tell about Baylor's beginnings as a chartered college in 1845. A particular story impressed me. It concerned an affluent businessman, Mr. Francis Carroll. In a season of prosperity, he donated $25,000 for the construction of one of Baylor's first academic buildings. At the time of this gift, $25,000 was a huge sum of money. Later on, however, Mr. Carroll suffered great financial losses. During this period of hardship, he and a friend stood on campus and looked at the building named after him. He turned to his friend and said, "The only thing I have left is what I gave away." Nothing could be more true. The only thing you take with you to heaven is what you give away on earth!

WHAT

Let's move on now to answer the question, "what?" What exactly do we give financially to the Lord? Three biblical words or expressions define what money we give to God: firstfruits, tithe, and offerings.

Firstfruits

Solomon stood out as the wisest man on earth during his lifetime. He wrote, "Honor the Lord with your wealth, with the firstfruits of all your crops" (Proverbs 3:9). The firstfruits denote the first part of what you gain from your work. You honor God in a special way when you give back to Him the first portion of income He has privileged you to manage. You don't offer God what is left over, after you pay the bills. This would dishonor Him, like giving left-overs from the refrigerator to an honorable guest in your home.

Our family budget lists many areas of expenses such as house payment, groceries, utilities, and car insurance. But the item at the top of our budget is firstfruits. We give to God first, before we do any-thing else with the family income. This shows that we seriously accept responsibility of the command to honor the Lord with the firstfruits of our wages.

What amount of money do you actually designate as the firstfruits to God? The answer appears in the Old Testament book of Malachi, which points out the necessity of presenting a tithe to the Lord. A tithe means 10 percent. Let's consider the tithe, the next key word for "what" we give to the Lord.

Tithe

"Bring the whole tithe into the storehouse ..." (Malachi 3:10). A tithe is the first 10 percent of your income, given to God before any personal expenses. Prioritize the tithe above every expenditure and obligation. Why? Because the firstfruits, the first 10 percent of income, honors the Lord in direct obedience to His Word.

In the Old Testament, the tithes of the Israelites met three needs. They furnished the feasts and worship events (Deuteronomy 14:23), compensated the priests and Levites who led worship and instructed the people (Numbers 18:21), and supplied the needs of the aliens, widows, and orphans (Deuteronomy 26:12-13).

The tithes of God's people today parallel the three original purposes in the Old Testament. First, they support the local church, its worship services, meetings, events, ministries, and outreach. Second, the tithes pay the salaries of church leadership. Third, tithes assist the poor, both locally and globally.

If all Christians would tithe, every need of the church, every need of its leadership, and every need of the poor would be met. Tithing is God's straightforward plan to fulfill all needs. He provides 100 percent of your income by His grace, blessing you with a job and paycheck. Then He asks you, and all Christians, for 10 percent of it back. The total amount cares for all the needs of the church and the poor. What a simple and profound plan!

It might be tempting to think you can't afford to tithe when you earn a small paycheck. I know that train of thought. I was unemployed twice and had little or no income. However, I'm glad I didn't buy in to that temptation. I determined to honor the Lord and help, albeit little, to meet the needs of God's people and the poor. Although small in amount, my tithe exalted God as much as someone who tithed out of a large salary. And as I honored Him, He met all my needs.

It may also be tempting to think you can't afford to tithe when you earn substantial wages. Possibly you have elevated your standard of living, owning a bigger house, driving a more expensive vehicle, or vacationing more luxuriously. How can you tithe when you face these financial obligations? The answer is elementary: Change your obligations! Place the significance of tithing (to honor the Lord and meet the needs of the church and the poor) over and above your chosen lifestyle. You might lower your expenses by selling a car, spending less, or even moving into a smaller home.

Offerings

Offerings are monies given to God over and above the tithe or the first 10 percent of your income. At times, special needs warrant such generosity. For example, in the early church many Christians in Jerusalem lived in poverty. The apostle Paul organized a team effort to collect offerings from various churches and then transport the money to those in financial distress. These offerings flowed out of compassionate hearts that cared for fellow Christians.

Scripture describes the serious nature of giving a tithe and offerings: "Will a man rob God? Yet you rob me. But you ask, 'How do we rob you?' In tithes and offerings" (Malachi 3:8). God is robbed of honor when a Christian does not give as the Bible prescribes. Why? Because the believer views God as untrustworthy. He steals away reverence and respect from God. The Lord is not recognized as Lord, the Source and Owner of all. Holding back the tithe and offerings goes beyond selfishness. It is spiritual robbery.

My wife and I sit down at the beginning of each year to establish our family budget for the next 12 months. We total our expected income for the year. Then we figure 10 percent of that gross income as the tithe. Next we determine how much we will give, over and above our tithe, to special projects within our church. Last, we itemize people or organizations, outside of our church, we deem worthy of our financial support. Anything over and above the tithe, whether given within the church or outside the church, is called an offering.

WHERE

The next question is "where" do you give the tithe to honor God? The Bible instructs: "Bring the whole tithe into the storehouse, that there may be food in my house..." (Malachi 3:10). The Old Testament storehouse refers to the temple treasury, equivalent to the finances of today's local church. You place the tithe in the treasury of your fellowship so all the needs of the church, its leaders, and the poor might be met.

You may want to contribute offerings for special or unforeseen needs, whether in your fellowship or outside the church. However, this money should not be taken out of the tithe, which is reserved and dedicated to honor the Lord through your church home. Unfortunately, some Christians distribute their tithe (or part of their tithe) to individuals, ministries, or various organizations. Consequently, the church suffers as the storehouse or treasury dips low. The result? The fellowship cannot provide sufficient funds for ministries or missions. The church may not be positioned financially to compensate its leaders adequately, and the concerns of the poor might be left unaddressed as well. The church just can't do all God desires unless everyone brings the entire tithe into the storehouse of the fellowship.

WHEN

How frequently will the tithe be given? No hard and fast rule exists about frequency. Some give their tithe weekly, some do so monthly. Others tithe when they get paid, letting their check serve as a built-in reminder of God's goodness, and that it's time again to honor Him for His blessings. Consistency is the most important factor. Simply figure out a time to tithe regularly and stick to it. God will be pleased.

Whatever you do, don't put off consistent giving of your firstfruits. It is just too tempting to withhold the tithe because of mounting bills, unforeseen expenses, or unwise spending. When Paul collected the offerings for the needy Christians in Jerusalem he advised the churches to have people set aside an amount weekly, in keeping with their income. If offerings were set aside weekly, how much more the tithe should be dedicated to the Lord on a regular basis.

HOW

The final question is "how?" How should your heart respond in the process of giving tithes and offerings? The Bible encourages a heart that gives cheerfully, generously, and expectantly.

Cheerfully

The attitude of your heart rejoices in the opportunity to honor the Lord through financial giving.

"Each man should give what he has decided in his heart to give, not reluctantly or under compulsion, for God loves a cheerful giver" (2 Corinthians 9:7). The tithe and offerings you present to God come out of cheerfulness, not compulsion. You know how much God has given for you, especially the sacrifice of Christ to pay the penalty for your sins. So giving 10 percent or more of your money to Him arises out of joy, not obligation. Giving a tithe and offerings is not a burden. Rather, it is a privilege to honor the Lord who gave everything for you.

I incurred significant debt a couple times as a Christian. During those times I found it easy to think, "It's impossible to give the firstfruits cheerfully to God." However, I learned that even during these seasons cheerful giving is possible, as well as the right thing to do. Debt does not change the biblical commands concerning tithes and offerings. Furthermore, consistent giving puts you in a better position to pay off obligations because you are working with God, not against Him. Give cheerfully, then, whatever your financial circumstances.

Generously

One day Jesus watched a number of rich people place their monetary gifts in the temple treasury. In contrast, a poor widow came along and put in two very small coins. Jesus commended the widow for contributing more than all the others combined, because she sacrificed the last two coins she possessed. The poor widow powerfully modeled generosity, for she gave out of her poverty, whereas others gave out of their wealth (Luke 21:1-4).

God loves cheerful giving. Add generosity to cheerfulness, and God commends you, like the widow. You stand out as an example for others to follow. Generous giving, of course, is not restricted to sacrificing your last two pennies. It includes any act of giving beyond the norm of consistent tithes and offerings. Therefore, stay big-hearted and open-handed, letting God raise you up as an example of generosity.

Expectantly

Expect God to meet all your needs as you give cheerfully and generously. The scripture declares: "... Whoever sows sparingly will also reap sparingly, and whoever sows generously will also reap generously" (2 Corinthians 9:6). The amount of seed a farmer plants in the soil normally predicts the size of his harvest. The same is true with sowing finances into God's church and its ministries. The more you give, the more you will likely receive.

Generosity eliminates worry about personal or family needs, then, simply because you cannot out-give God! He pours out more blessing on you than you could ever extend toward Him. "... Then your barns will be filled to overflowing, and your vats will brim over with new wine" (Proverbs 3:10). In addition, always remember that He gave you Jesus. Therefore, won't your gracious heavenly Father meet your earthly needs as well?

Three qualifications are appropriate here. First, I do not promote a "give to get" mentality, for any self-centered approach to giving contradicts its true nature. More significantly, the Bible does not teach giving as a means to enrich ourselves or accumulate wealth for selfish reasons.

Secondly, exceptions exist to the sowing and reaping principle. For example, persecuted Christians throughout history have not been rewarded on earth for their generosity and sacrifice in the material realm. Their rewards are far better, purely eternal, reserved in heaven.

Third, God multiplies blessing back to us when we give so we have more to share with others. "Now he who supplies seed to the sower and bread for food will also supply and increase your store of seed and will enlarge the harvest of your righteousness. You will be made rich in every way so that you can be generous on every occasion ..." (2 Corinthians 9:10-11). God delights to bless His generous children and no embarrassment should accompany the possession of material wealth. At the same time, the primary purpose of financial blessing is to grow as a cheerful, generous person on every occasion.

My Story

In 1986, my wife and I started a church in our home with two other couples. My beginning salary totaled $500/month, the exact amount of our house payment. Obviously, we didn't have enough money for groceries and other necessities. One day our finances dipped to an all-time low of $29. A famine persisted in another country at that time, and I sensed the Lord speaking to my heart. He asked me to give our last dollars away to the starving children of that nation, even though our pantry was bare. When I told my wife, she agreed. Now we had nothing, but really we had everything, most notably the God who gives generously and blesses those who sow generously. And so He did. We continued with the $500/month income for some time, but not one bill went unpaid or paid late. God opened the supernatural faucet of His generosity. Money came to us from surprising sources. Why? Because we continued to give even when in need ourselves. Be a cheerful and generous giver and you can expect God to meet your every need.

Here are seven practical ways to help you become a faithful money manager.

1. **Establish a realistic budget**.
   Key question: Do I know how my income is being spent?
2. **Give tithes and offerings regularly**.
   Key question: Am I honoring the Lord consistently with my money?
3. **Pray about every major purchase**.
   Key question: Is this item God's will?
4. **Borrow only for appreciable items, like a home or a college education**.
   Key question: Is this a good investment?
5. **Distinguish between wants and needs**.
   Key question: How much is enough?

6. **Laugh at commercials and ads that tempt you to spend unwisely.**
   Key question: Are you kidding me?!
7. **Increase annually the percentage of your giving.**
   Key question: How does God want me to be generous?

Application Questions
for Chapter 10 — Finances

1. For you, what is the most significant reason for giving money to God through the church?

2. Why do a large majority of Christians not give the first 10% of their income to the Lord?

3. In your estimation, is tithing easier when you have a smaller income or larger income?

4. How does love for God relate to financial giving?

5. Have you ever given a tithe or offering without a cheerful heart? If so, what were the circumstances?

6. If people fully believed God would meet all their material needs, what might their giving look like?

7. To establish consistent and cheerful giving of your tithes and offerings to God through your church, what would need to change? Map out a plan to reach this goal.

Chapter 11

Witnessing

Extending the Truth of Christ

"The church is the only cooperative society in the world that exists for the benefit of its non-members." Bishop William Temple

Financial giving honors God, supports the church, and supplies the needs of the poor. It is absolutely necessary. The greatest form of giving, though, is letting others hear, see, and experience the reality of Christ through you, as you live out Christianity day to day. Therefore, let's delve into the practical ways of extending the truth of Christ to those around us.

Jesus said to his earliest disciples, "...you will receive power when the Holy Spirit comes on you; and you will be my witnesses ..." (Acts 1:8). A witness tells what he observes. For instance, if you view an accident you may be called by a court of law as a witness. If so, you simply tell others what you saw. Your report discloses a first-hand experience or account of the circumstances.

The same is true spiritually. You are an eyewitness to the reality of Jesus Christ. When you encounter His love, you are responsible to let others know about your repentance, water baptism, receiving the Holy Spirit's power, discovery of God's will, perseverance through temptations and trials, etc. You just tell what you experienced. This personal story is often referred to as a testimony. You convey your testimony, or witness, in three ways — through message, model, and ministry. All three modes of witnessing are fundamental to authentic Christianity, since a believer is expected to extend the truth of Christ to others.

Message

The message outlines the content of the gospel. You communicate the good news that Jesus came to earth as God in flesh. You tell how He died on a cross, taking the punishment for your sins. You convey the story of how Christ captured your heart and now reigns as your King. This message forms your testimony that Jesus is Savior and Lord of your life. Some people will not like the message. Others may even take personal offense, rejecting the message and possibly you as well. Be encouraged, for this rejection is not really about you. Jesus said, "If the world hates you, keep in mind that it hated me first" (John 15:18).

A Christian friend of mine endured this type of rejection while employed at a hospital in our hometown. He often found open doors to articulate his testimony as he looked for opportunities to extend the truth of Christ at work. But the hospital administration heard of his pattern of witnessing and asked him to stop speaking about Jesus. My friend was an exemplary worker with a high probability of future promotions. However, he knew that muzzling the message of Jesus would compromise his obedience to God. So he continued to share his faith in Christ with fellow workers.

As a result, he lost all chance for career advancement. However, many hospital employees came to repentance and discovered a new life in Jesus. The spiritual rewards far outweighed the positional and financial rewards he would have received by silencing his witness. Fifteen years later, my friend received a job offer from another hospital. He benefited not only from a substantial pay increase, but also from a huge promotion, the highest possible within his field of medicine! God rewarded him spiritually and then, at a later time, monetarily.

From this true story you can recognize the cost of faithfully witnessing to others. In fact, the New Testament Greek word for witness is *martus*, the word from which we derive our English word, martyr. A witness sacrifices himself for the higher cause of the gospel. Few may be required to literally die for their faith, but all Christians must be ready to sacrifice any type of personal gain or popularity for the greater value of sharing the life-transforming message of Jesus Christ.

Therefore, expect opposition and remain patient. God will give you courage, whenever necessary, to die to personal preferences, hopes, and desires. He will reveal the light of Christ through the communication of your testimony, giving witness of His grace-filled message. And in the proper season, God will bless you for extending the truth of Christ.

Model

Whereas the witness of the message happens primarily through verbal communication, the witness of your model occurs primarily through exemplary living. People recognize the Christian values you practice such as prayer, Bible study, and fellowship. Some may notice how you honor God with your money. You also model authentic Christianity through a positive attitude, refusal to participate in impure conversations, a strong work ethic, respect for authority, etc. Walking these godly avenues is living your testimony. You model the message for those who don't follow Jesus. Your character and behavior speak volumes without using words.

Jesus encouraged His disciples to be a model when He said, "… Love one another. As I have loved you, so you must love one another. By this all men will know that you are my disciples, if you love one another" (John 13:34-35). The love you share with other Christians is, in itself, a standard that reveals Christ.

For example, many years ago my wife and I met Karen, a young lady who visited our church. She was an engineer — single, smart, and successful. We became better acquainted with her when she attended a young adult group at our home. She appeared to be "checking out" Christianity, prompted by the godly lifestyle of a friend who invited her. Startled by the love we had for one another in the church, Karen felt accepted and reached out for a life that previously seemed unattainable.

One day she called me, asking for an appointment at the church office. Upon arrival, she confessed her sexual involvement with her boyfriend (also not a Christian). Then she reported the likelihood of being pregnant, and requested my input on the possibility of an abortion. I gently, but firmly, asserted that an abortion would be the wrong choice.

Karen didn't seem surprised by my response. In fact, her recent attentiveness to the godly lifestyle of her Christian friend, and the love she observed in our fellowship, awakened a desire in her heart to follow Jesus. She longed to embrace the model she saw in the church. Karen eagerly desired to do the right thing, even as she sat in my office with huge decisions in front of her.

At this point, I issued an invitation to give control of her life to the Lord. This was her turning point. Karen repented and became a new person in Christ. When she left my office she no longer contemplated the end of her baby's life. Rather, she rejoiced that she herself had new life through Christ.

Soon thereafter, Karen discovered she was not pregnant after all. She also broke up with her boyfriend. As she matured in her faith, I asked her to help lead the young adult group. A few years later she married a Christian man. Both she and her husband left their jobs and enrolled in a Christian graduate school, obtaining masters degrees in counseling. Together they started a Christian counseling center.

I attribute these wonderful changes to the love Karen saw in her Christian friend and our church. What amazing things God can do as we demonstrate the reality of Christ, modeling the Lord's compassion.

Ministry

Message expresses the content of the gospel. Model reflects the lifestyle of the gospel. Ministry depicts the outreach of the gospel. What do I mean by outreach? I mean intentional acts of kindness aimed at extending the truth of Christ to others.

For example, a woman invites neighbors to a "ladies' coffee" to get acquainted and inform them of a Bible study she would like to start. Soon ten women gather weekly to enjoy coffee and conversation, and learn about God's plan for their lives. Ministry like this is intentional and powerful as a witness of Jesus Christ.

Sometimes the simple act of praying for someone who is sick opens a door for the gospel. The New Testament book of Acts contains at least four scenarios where this transpired: Acts 3:1-10; 8:4-13; 9:32-35; 9:36-43. Let's look at Acts 9:32-35.

³²*As Peter traveled about the country, he went to visit the saints in Lydda.* ³³*There he found a man named Aeneas, a paralytic who had been bedridden for eight years.* ³⁴ *"Aeneas," Peter said to him, "Jesus Christ heals you. Get up and take care of your mat." Immediately Aeneas got up.* ³⁵*All those who lived in Lydda and Sharon saw him and turned to the Lord.*

The apostle Peter encountered a paralytic named Aeneas, who was bedridden for eight years. After Aeneas was healed through Peter's intentional outreach, two villages turned to the Lord. What an explosion of the gospel throughout that area after one simple gesture of compassion!

Stay sensitive to ministry opportunities. Consider how to bless those who live or work near you. If someone at work is ill, how might you approach them to pray for their healing? Frequent opportunities emerge at unpredictable times. Be prepared, keep the eyes of your heart open, and rejoice as God makes ways to represent Him in ministry. Whatever you do, do something. For example, maybe you could take the sick person a meal or write an encouraging note. Then watch for further occasion to communicate the message and demonstrate the model.

A primary means for witnessing through ministry is the use of your spiritual gifts. For example, I went to the golf course recently to practice at the chipping green. Another man practiced nearby. I could see out of my peripheral vision that he struggled consistently with his chip shot. Soon, he inquired how to hit the ball properly. I offered some quick instruction and he changed his method. As he tried the new swing I demonstrated, he began to have new difficulties. I hung around for a while to encourage him. About 30 minutes later, he started stroking the ball solidly and accurately. He thanked me numerous times for his improved shot-making ability.

Looking back, it dawned on me that I was utilizing my spiritual gifts of teaching and encouragement, regardless of how mundane the context. No wonder it took relatively little time to instruct him and bless him (and hopefully help his golf score)! Of greater importance, I spoke with him more personally before leaving the golf course. I also invited him to church. His departing comment indicated he would come and bring his family. This interaction with a complete stranger typifies the use of spiritual gifts as ministry at any time and in any place.

Do you see the correlation between the most elementary form of kindness and the spiritual openness that results? Do you notice how the most simplistic use of spiritual gifts can be a ministry that potentially extends the truth of Christ to others? Reach out, then, taking healthy advantage of day-to-day openings to show compassion. Your ministry will not be in vain.

No one is excused or disqualified from witnessing. Consider Timothy, the young man in the New Testament who was mentored by the apostle Paul. Timothy struggled with shyness and fear. As a result, Paul consistently encouraged him to "preach the word" (2 Timothy 4:2) and "do the work of an evangelist" (2 Timothy 4:5). Even though Timothy was challenged by feelings of cowardice, he could not neglect the responsibility of presenting the message, model, and ministry.

What about you? Do you welcome opportunities to represent your Savior and Lord to a world that desperately needs Him? Timothy rose to the occasion. You can as well. Let me provide a few practical guidelines to assist you in reaching out as a witness.

1. **Time** – Take time to get acquainted with those around you who need the Savior, including neighbors, co-workers, and classmates.

2. **Interest** – Show interest in those with whom you interact. Ask them pertinent questions. Follow up on conversations. Pray for them to be receptive to the love of Jesus.

3. **Kindness** – Reveal kindness in your words and actions. After all, God's kindness leads people toward repentance (Romans 2:4). Therefore, listen well. Share opinions discreetly and respectfully. Never condemn. Serve people with intentional acts of caring. Be available for those unpredictable moments to pray for someone or meet a practical need.

4. **Focus** – Maintain focus on the goal of witnessing by verbalizing the message, demonstrating the model, and implementing the ministry of Jesus. Be encouraged as you pursue this goal. You don't need to know all the answers to questions you receive. You don't have to conduct a perfect lifestyle to represent Christ well. And you certainly aren't required to serve others in any preconceived

way. Be who God has made you, and you'll naturally find yourself extending the truth of Christ to others.

Application Questions
for Chapter 11 — Witnessing

1. Who verbally conveyed the message of Christ, helping you in the process of becoming a Christian? How did they introduce the subject of Jesus? What was your initial response?

2. Who did you consider a model of the Christian life? What qualities did they represent that attracted you to Jesus?

3. Did someone reach out in ministry (before you came to repentance), showing God's love in a way that impacted you for the Lord? If so, explain.

4. What is the primary avenue by which you've shared your faith in Jesus . . . message, model, or ministry? Give an illustration and tell how the person responded.

5. Articulate your greatest challenge to represent Christ as a witness to unbelievers.

Chapter 12

Worship

Honoring the Person of Christ

"Authentic Christianity is not learning a set of doctrines ... It is a walk – a supernatural walk with a living, dynamic, communicating God."
Bill Hybels

Witnessing and worshipping go hand in hand. Witnessing honors God by extending the love of Christ. Worshipping honors God by expressing love to Christ. Witness moves outward. Worship flows upward.

Meaning of Worship

Worship means to honor God. Christians gather consistently to sing songs and hymns of praise to honor God in what are commonly called worship services. But honoring God encompasses more than gatherings in a church sanctuary (or fellowship groups in a home). A person of authentic Christianity worships God in every aspect of life — thoughts, attitudes, words, and actions. In addition, honoring God involves every arena of life — home, work, school, and neighborhood. This chapter will address worship, then, from both a worship service context and an overall life perspective.

Reasons for Worship

First things first, however: Why do you worship God? Because of who He is! The Bible says, "Great is the Lord, and most worthy of praise …" (Psalm 48:1); "… the Lord is faithful to all his promises and loving toward all he has made" (Psalm 145:13). God deserves worship because of all His wonderful attributes, such as greatness, faithfulness, love, etc.

You worship God, as well, because of what He has done. Scripture says, "But you are a chosen people, a royal priesthood, a holy nation, a people belonging to God, that you may declare the praises of him who called you out of darkness into his wonderful light" (1 Peter 2:9). God ransomed you as His own child through the sacrifice of Jesus, who died to forgive you of sin and release you into a new life of righteousness. You are chosen! You belong to God! You are part of His family, the church! You no longer walk in spiritual darkness! Honoring the person of Christ is a natural response to what He has done. If

God never did anything else for you, salvation alone warrants worship every day the rest of your life.

Attitude for Worship

Humility summarizes the necessary attitude to worship God, because you cannot honor God and exalt yourself simultaneously. Pride and worship are mutually exclusive. Jesus painted an explicit picture of the need for humility in the parable of the Pharisee and tax collector:

> [9]*To some who were confident of their own righteousness and looked down on everybody else, Jesus told this parable:* [10]*"Two men went up to the temple to pray, one a Pharisee and the other a tax collector.* [11]*The Pharisee stood up and prayed about himself: 'God, I thank you that I am not like other men — robbers, evildoers, adulterers — or even like this tax collector.* [12]*I fast twice a week and give a tenth of all I get.'*
> [13]*"But the tax collector stood at a distance. He would not even look up to heaven, but beat his breast and said, 'God, have mercy on me, a sinner.'*
> [14]*"I tell you that this man, rather than the other, went home justified before God. For everyone who exalts himself will be humbled, and he who humbles himself will be exalted." (Luke 18:9-14)*

Both men entered the temple for the purpose of prayer, which is obviously a form of worship. The Pharisee prayed in a self-centered and self-congratulatory fashion. Meanwhile, the tax collector looked down in lowliness of spirit, confessing his sin. The conclusion? The tax collector left the temple affirmed as a genuine worshipper whereas the Pharisee faced the prospect of God's discipline. Look more closely at the stark contrast between these two men:

Condition of Heart

Pharisee:	Arrogance
Tax Collector:	Reverence

Source of Satisfaction

Pharisee:	Self
Tax Collector:	God

Sense of Awareness

Pharisee:	Personal Virtues
Tax Collector:	Personal Needs

Focus of Relationship

Pharisee:	Compared Self to Others
Tax Collector:	Submitted Self to God

Posture before God

Pharisee:	Stood Up to be Seen
Tax Collector:	Stood Aside to Pray

Goal of Worship

Pharisee:	Exalt Self & Get Attention
Tax Collector:	Honor God & Seek Mercy

Response of God

Pharisee:	Discipline (Humbled)
Tax Collector:	Approval (Justified)

Unless you accept your ongoing need for God, you will assume a self-righteous stance like the

Pharisee. On the other hand, continually embracing your dependence on God's mercy will breed a humble attitude essential to true worship. Therefore, humble yourself before the Lord and let Him lift you up (James 4:10).

Simplicity of Worship

Humility makes genuine worship not only possible, but simple. It's all about Him, and not about you. For example, Jesus visited two sisters, Mary and Martha. Mary dropped everything to worship the Lord, but Martha felt obligated to do all the domestic chores related to entertaining Jesus in their home. Luke 10 records this story:

[38]*As Jesus and his disciples were on their way, he came to a village where a woman named Martha opened her home to him.* [39]*She had a sister called Mary, who sat at the Lord's feet listening to what he said.* [40]*But Martha was distracted by all the preparations that had to be made. She came to him and asked, "Lord, don't you care that my sister has left me to do the work by myself? Tell her to help me!"*

[41]*"Martha, Martha," the Lord answered, "you are worried and upset about many things,* [42]*but only one thing is needed. Mary has chosen what is better, and it will not be taken away from her."*

Simplicity distinguished Mary from Martha. Mary sat at the feet of Jesus listening (a form of worship), but Martha complicated matters. First, she distracted herself from worship by undue concern about hospitable preparations. Second, she questioned the Lord's heart of caring related to the amount of work she was doing. Third, she grew unnecessarily angry with her sister, who continued listening to the Lord. Finally, Martha ordered Jesus to get Mary busy with the housework!

Then "… the Lord answered, you are worried and upset about many things …" (vs. 41). Martha had a "many-things complex." She obsessed about the numerous responsibilities she perceived as imperative. On the other hand, Mary would not let anything deter her from worship. Martha modeled complexity; Mary displayed simplicity. As a result, Jesus corrected Martha saying, "… only one thing is needed. Mary has chosen what is better …" (vss. 41-42). Mary, the sister with whom Martha was angry, possessed the very thing Martha needed — the simplicity of worship!

It's certainly commendable to work diligently. But Martha overdid responsibility to the expense of her relationship with Jesus. In society today the "many-things complex" remains a continual temptation, particularly for organized and/or conscientious types of people. Let me encourage you to honor the person of Christ, every day and all day. Don't allow anything or anyone to prevent or distract you from worshipping.

Simplicity of worship relates to daily life. More particularly, it applies to worship services at your church (or in a small group or private worship). How easily "things" come to the forefront of the mind, pulling focus away from honoring the Lord. Personally, I've encountered distraction more times than I'd like to admit. After 34 years of worshipping God, I am still learning to ignore the "urgent concerns" that attempt to lure me away from the better thing of honoring the person of Christ with full concentration. Consider the following ways which have helped me maintain a worship focus:

- Close your eyes to block out visual distractions.
- Write down mental diversions for later consideration.
- Engage in one of the many biblical worship expressions such as kneeling (Psalm 95:6, Luke 22:41), bowing (2 Chronicles 29:28, Psalm 5:7), or raising hands to God (Psalm 134:2, 1 Timothy 2:8).

Authentic Christianity consistently shows reverence for Jesus Christ. Therefore, worship privately, in small fellowship groups, in large church gatherings, and in everyday life from one moment to the next. Honor God at all times and in all places. Be like Mary, and choose the simplicity of worship.

Intimacy in Worship

When humility and simplicity unite, closeness with God results. With a clean heart and clear focus you can expect to worship Him in wonderful intimacy. The scripture says, "Let us draw near to God with a sincere heart in full assurance of faith

…" (Hebrews 10:22). Sincere indicates a single purpose. As defined earlier, the sole purpose of worship is honoring the person of Christ. When you honor Him, He honors you. How? By lifting you into ever-increasing heights of relationship, wherein He reveals His nature and purpose. Worship, then, is a two-way street. You communicate to God in prayer and praise, and He replies back to you. I call this reciprocal nature of intimacy in worship "expression and impression." You express your heart to God and He impresses His heart on you. You tell the Lord how much you love Him, and He conveys His perfect and unconditional love for you. Intimacy!

Joelle is our second child. As a toddler, she would often stand in front of me with hands raised and say, "Hold you, Daddy." She meant, of course, "Hold me, Daddy." I would pick her up and hold her, and Joelle would hold me in her sweet toddler fashion. She definitely understood the child-father relationship was reciprocal, a back and forth blessing of one another. This illustrates worship. You stand before the Lord, draw close to Him, and He lifts you up to bless you. He blesses you with His closeness as you bless Him with yours. You express love to Him, and He impresses love on you. Wow! Authentic Christianity is real, meaningful, life-giving relationship with your eternal Daddy.

Many life-giving impressions transpire on this two-way street of spiritual intimacy in worship. God may comfort you, restore your perspective, remind you of His faithfulness, expose a scheme of Satan, lift a burden, convict you of a sin, flood you with

His peace, or bring an encouraging scripture to mind. Listening to God in worship is paramount, then. Expression plus impression form an intimate dialogue of our spirit with God's Spirit. Expression alone is incomplete worship, just as a one-way conversation with a close friend is incomplete communication.

In this sense, worship is analogous to giving. As seen in Chapter 10, God blesses the financial giving of tithes and offerings. He answers through His law of sowing and reaping. When you sow generously you reap generously. So it is with worship. As you draw near to honor God with time, praise, and adoration, He responds in ways that bless you. So you can joyfully anticipate meeting personally with God in all contexts of worship.

At the same time, worship does not prioritize getting something from God. Just as we don't give money to grasp for riches, we don't worship to clutch for God's blessings. God blesses as He so chooses, not because we have jumped through some "spiritual hoop." In genuine humility, however, be assured whenever you "come near to God ..., He will come near to you" (James 4:8).

Result of Worship

Worship produces purity. How could it not? Anyone who humbly, intentionally, and sincerely honors the person of Christ will mature in purity, growing further and further into the holiness of the One worshipped. People instinctively become like the one they honor.

Our daughter, Joelle, is especially passionate about worship. She considers her daily time alone with God quite seriously. She pursues intimacy with the Lord in small groups and church services as well. In addition, Joelle perceives worship as a lifestyle that honors God, much more than compartments of time to pray and sing. The result of her worshipful life reflects purity.

For instance, Joelle participated on a prestigious team of dancers. They practiced daily and entertained at various locations and events. She loved it, and enjoyed both her team and coaches. But then a quandary arose. Questionable dance moves began to appear in the choreography. In good conscience, she couldn't perform in any dance that contained such movements. With the approval and acceptance of the coaches, Joelle sat out each dance that could have easily put a stumbling block or obstacle in her brother's way (Romans 14:13). Eventually she found it necessary to step down from this great team. Like anything else, if her dancing did not honor God she would set it aside.

Do you see how a heart of worship produces purity? The apostle Paul wrote to the Christians in Rome, "Therefore, I urge you, brothers, in view of God's mercy, to offer your bodies as living sacrifices, holy and pleasing to God — this is your spiritual act of worship" (Romans 12:1). Worship encircles everything you are and everything you do. Every aspect of life is meant to be a sacrifice, holy and pleasing to God. And why not? After all, your God is filled with mercy. The life you enjoy as a Christian is evidence. Therefore, stay strong in view of God's mercy, even as you started strong.

Application Questions
for Chapter 12 — Worship

1. Why is God worthy of worship?

2. What attitude easily inhibits worship?

3. What distracts you in worship settings with others? In worship times alone? What helps you regain a focus of worship?

4. Have you experienced intimacy with God in worship wherein you not only expressed your love to Him, but He also impressed His love on you? If so, share a way this has occurred and the effect it had on you.

5. Ultimately, worship means to honor God. In what ways do you exhibit a lifestyle of worship?

Conclusion

*"We have come to share in Christ if we hold
firmly till the end the confidence we had at first."
(Hebrews 3:14)*

I want you to start strong in your Christian life and
stay strong in Christ for the long haul. Jesus said,
"… He who stands firm to the end will be saved"
(Matthew 24:13). Unfortunately, many falter along
the way and become spiritual casualties instead of
spiritual conquerors. In the parable of the sower,
Jesus told a story about those who stand firm to the
end, in contrast to those who do not.

*⁴While a large crowd was gathering and people
were coming to Jesus from town after town, he told
this parable: ⁵ "A farmer went out to sow his seed. As
he was scattering the seed, some fell along the path;
it was trampled on, and the birds of the air ate it up.
⁶Some fell on rock, and when it came up, the plants
withered because they had no moisture. ⁷Other seed*

fell among thorns, which grew up with it and choked the plants. [8]Still other seed fell on good soil. It came up and yielded a crop, a hundred times more than was sown."

When he said this, he called out, "He who has ears to hear, let him hear." ...

[11]*"This is the meaning of the parable: The seed is the word of God. [12]Those along the path are the ones who hear, and then the devil comes and takes away the word from their hearts, so that they may not believe and be saved. [13]Those on the rock are the ones who receive the word with joy when they hear it, but they have no root. They believe for a while, but in the time of testing they fall away. [14]The seed that fell among thorns stands for those who hear, but as they go on their way they are choked by life's worries, riches and pleasures, and they do not mature. [15]But the seed on good soil stands for those with a noble and good heart, who hear the word, retain it, and by persevering produce a crop." (Luke 8:4-8, 11-15)*

This parable describes four different people. The first person hears the good news about Christ, but does not believe it. The devil introduces doubt, fear or some other factor to harden his heart. This prohibits him from getting started as a Christian because the seed of the gospel never penetrates his spirit.

The second person hears the gospel message and responds with joy. However, his belief is temporary. He falls away from authentic Christianity when troubles arise and his faith is tested. Surely he likes the idea of becoming a Christian in order to have eternal life. But he has not experienced a genuine turnaround. He is into Christianity for himself, not for Jesus. Therefore, he bails out when the waves of life's circumstances crash against him.

The third person also accepts the good news temporarily. He might grow spiritually for awhile, but then worries, desires, or pleasures reassume priority. Godly values that began to germinate are choked out by worldly values. So, he never develops a mature relationship with Jesus. He eventually drops out of the Christian race long before the finish line.

The fourth person hears the truth about Jesus, then secures it in his heart. He is like good soil retaining the life of a seed. He does not just believe in Christ. He is a real disciple, devoted to following the Lord regardless of what happens, refusing to be disillusioned by life's trials or derailed by worldly viewpoints. He is in the race not merely to run, but to finish and to finish strong. Therefore, he perseveres in all circumstances and lives a productive life yielded to God.

The apostle Paul was like the fourth person, the genuine disciple. Near the end of his life he said, "I have fought the good fight, I have finished the race, I have kept the faith" (2 Timothy 4:7). What will you say at the end of your time on earth? Which person will you be?

The biblical guidelines in this book will help you become like the fourth person in the parable. Satan may endeavor to steal away the truth of the gospel, but Jesus will win out. Trials may attempt to discourage you, but God will use them to mature you. Worries, riches, and pleasures may try to undermine your beliefs, but the Holy Spirit will strengthen you. With confidence, yield your heart to God, obey the Word of God, produce fruit for God, and persevere to the end! This is authentic Christianity: starting strong and staying strong.

9 781600 341205